eLIVate *Your Life*

7 Keys to spiritual and personal transformation

DR. Nona Djavid

and

Lani Baron ESQ.

www.eLIVateinstitute.com
Interior Graphics/Art Credit: MyChiroPractice Inc.

Cover design and interior design by Ardavan Javid / Graphicwise, Inc.

Balboa Press books may be ordered through booksellers or by contacting:

Balboa Press
A Division of Hay House
1663 Liberty Drive
Bloomington, IN 47403
www.balboapress.com
1 (877) 407-4847

Print information available on the last page.

ISBN: 978-1-5043-5547-6 (sc)
ISBN: 978-1-5043-5548-3 (e)

Balboa Press rev. date: 09/06/2016

Dedication

To my husband, for loving me for who I am; to my dad, for carrying me through fire; to my unborn daughter, for showing me the strength in allowing. – Lani

To my son Rayan - Nona

Contents

Introduction

How do you wake up every morning? Do you wake up next to the man or woman of your dreams? Are you surrounded by things you are proud of? Do you love your career? Do you spring out of bed excited for your day? Are you fulfilled? Even if you are happy, maybe you still find yourself wanting more out of life. As part of our growth as human beings, we will always find ourselves with the desire to become better with each passing day.

If you answered NO to any of these questions, it is time to STOP and evaluate your reason for being alive. If your WHY is not at the center of everything you do, and if you are not fulfilled in every aspect of your life, you are wasting the precious moments you have on this earth. These are the moments that were given to you. Each and every moment is a gift.

If you are reading this, you have already taken the first step to changing the course of your life.

eLIVate is a movement and a shift in the consciousness of the masses. We see too many people merely going through the motions of life; waking up, doing their routine, and repeating these motions over and over again with no passion. They feel in the grand scheme of things, their lives don't matter. We are here to tell you – you do matter. Your life has a purpose. We are going to show you how to find that purpose and live your truth. Today is the day those helpless, empty, and frustrated feelings leave you—for good.

There are probably a million reasons why you haven't harnessed your destiny. You might be fearful of failure, pushing your calling away because of obligations to your family, or you may just want to keep living a comfortable lifestyle with no challenge and no passion. The fact that you have picked up this book shows us that you're looking for something bigger. This shift in consciousness has been calling out to you, wanting you to take advantage of the knowledge that is now available to you.

Most of the concepts we talk about in this book are not new ideas, rather, Universal wisdoms that have been conveyed in many different books and lectures—echoed in each generation. After years of studying this information and applying it in our own lives, we can now show you how to use these pieces of wisdom, scattered throughout the eras of human existence, buried in the traditions of many different cultures the world over, and apply them to your own personal awakening.

We will teach you how to find your passion, your truth, your calling, how to align yourself, and allow you to make the biggest and best impact to improve your lifestyle, relationships, job, or whatever else you wish to change for the better.

We weren't always this tuned into the Light. There were moments in our own lives when we doubted ourselves, listened to our fears, and dreaded failure just like you. In this book, we share our stories; how we overcame those barriers and created the lives we wanted for ourselves—all by following the Light.

Who is writing this book?

> *"The Light at the end of the tunnel is no illusion; the tunnel is."*
>
> *– Unknown Author*

This book's voice is what we like to call the Light, but may also be referred to as "us" or "we," as it is the voice of our collective consciousness. This Light is inside everyone and can be found if you listen to it. You may call this voice your gut or intuition, and regardless if you've ever used it before to guide you through life, it has always been there and always will be. This voice is the one you hear inside your head even as you read these words. This very same voice pulls on your heart and gives you that sinking feeling in your stomach when something feels right or wrong. We decided to write this book from the Light's perspective. If anyone should motivate you to change your life, it should be the voice that knows you best.

How this book works

This book is laid out according to the acronym eLIVate. Each letter is a step on your journey, bringing you closer to a life full of joy, love, passion, and your inner truth. Each chapter will have information and exercises to help you get past the points of views that hold you back, and with each chapter you'll be one step closer to empowering yourself and listening your inner Light.

How the Light found us

We've had our fair share of adversity. When we met, we realized that there was one common denominator in the lives of all fulfilled people—mindset. The people who thrive in life are those who choose to do so. It has nothing to do with their backgrounds, education, upbringing, ethnicity, or gender. Instead, it has to do with how these people choose to govern their thoughts and their personal relationship with the Universe, to which we are all connected. We can choose to disconnect or reconnect at any moment. Our personal choice was to reconnect to this powerful and abundant force. We did so deliberately and continue to stay connected to it as a daily practice. As a result, we receive bits of inspiration that compel us to help others. Finding the Light is a personal choice. It is a decision your soul has been waiting for you to make, but one you must come to on your own. Our hope is that this book guides you back to the Light, where you were born and are meant to reside all of your life.

ENERGY

"The energy of the mind is the essence of life."
– Aristotle

"The geniuses have learned how to gather thought energy together to use for transforming their conceptions into material forms."
– Walter Russell

"This London City, with all its houses, palaces, steam-engines, cathedrals, and huge immeasurable traffic and tumult, what is it but a Thought, but millions of Thoughts made into One;—a huge immeasurable Spirit of a THOUGHT, embodied in brick, in iron, smoke, dust, Palaces, Parliaments, Hackney Coaches, Katherine Docks, and the rest of it! Not a brick was made but some man had to think of the making of that brick."
– Carlyle

As human beings, our nature is creative. As beings of Light and energy, we have the ability to use our thoughts, emotions and actions to co-create our lives with the Universe. We can connect our desire to manifest things when we feel a need or want. In these moments, we pull our vibrations to a level where our wants and needs can manifest themselves and the Universe responds. This force or energy is our essence as co-creators with the Universe (the Light). The challenge is to have the energy aligned with what we want around us at all times so we may co-create what we need when we need it. When we want or need something, that desire has come from our highest self. We will discuss this concept in more depth in the Alignment chapter of this book. For now, just know that no want or need is an accident.

You've probably already used your energy to manifest something before. Maybe your thoughts are drawn to a loved one or friend while driving in the car. Seconds later, the phone rings and it is the very person you were thinking of. Or, perhaps you need a certain amount of money to pay your monthly bills. Suddenly, a client or circumstance "just shows up" and brings you the exact needed amount. Some people like to call this coincidence, but we call this energy.

An Introduction to Energy

The technical definition of energy, as used in the physics field, is the capacity to do work. Energy is measured every day and with many actions we take without thinking. For example, a calorie found in the food we eat is a form of energy. The fuel we put in our cars is a form of energy. You are energy down to your very atoms. Knowing this, you can begin to understand your relationship to energy so you can direct it to create favorable outcomes in your life.

First, it is important to understand you can direct energy through the power of your thoughts, emotions, and beliefs. Here is an example:

There was an interesting study done where a group of scientists set up a test where protons were shot out of a gun and were aimed to hit a wall. They found that the photons actually changed direction based on where the test subjects were looking. When the test subjects looked at the protons, they went straight toward the wall. When they were not looking, the protons went in a completely different direction. The moral of the story is – energy follows your focus. Therefore, to create favorable outcomes in your life, you must always focus your energy where you want to go. A great way to think about this is to imagine yourself skiing. When you ski, it is important to look where you want to go. If you look straight ahead, your energy will be directed at your destination. If you look to the trees, however, you will end up by the trees.

How it Works

Before any of the myriad objects that surround us now was manifested into physical form, they were concepts in their creators' minds. For example, before you could sit in the chair underneath you right now, someone had to think of that chair—it was an idea. The person had to form a vision of what they wanted the chair to look like and make a plan for production. Finally, after manufacturing, the chair came into existence in our physical world; energy at work.

Basically, you, and everyone else, have a "vibrational bubble" of energy surrounding you at all times. As you go through the day, your thoughts get caught in and start to circle around your vibrational bubble and become heavy as they accumulate more and more energy. Finally, these thoughts become so heavy they must land in the physical world in some form. This is how circumstances and events end up in our lives.

The words used to describe this may seem new to you, but you have experienced this phenomenon many times before whether you recognized it or not. Have you ever walked into a room filled with people and described it as, "full of energy?" What about when you liked someone and got along with him just fine, until someone told you something negative about that person? The person who brought negative behavior to your attention just drew this energy into your vibrational bubble. They have shifted your perspective on the person, and therefore your focus. Now, you can't help but notice this behavior, and wonder how you missed it before.

Another example of this is when you have a great idea or even a joke that you think is really funny. You may describe your idea to someone you trust with lots of energy, and this person gives you a feeling that the idea is not as great as you thought. Suddenly, you feel a drop in energy—a sinking feeling. This is an example of how your thoughts have energy. Finally, have you ever been thinking of someone only to look down at your phone and see them calling or texting you? It's because you focused your energy on this person and therefore attracted them. Feel free to test this concept out. Next time you are out and about, make it your goal to look for yellow cars. You may think this is such an uncommon color for a car, but you'll be surprised how many you'll start to count. This isn't because there are more cars on the road; it is because you have now programmed your mind to notice them. When you place a thought into your vibrational bubble, it will begin to show up in your physical world.

The tricky part here is monitoring our thoughts and understanding their relationship with time. Many thoughts in our vibrational bubble are not ones we want to land in our laps. In addition, many thoughts that are forming our reality, even now, will not manifest into physical form right away. This depends on the strength of the thought. A thought becomes strong when it is coupled with desire and emotion. When this occurs, the thought manifests itself into the physical world much faster.

Therefore, to manifest the things you want (or avoid manifesting what you don't want), keep the following formula in mind:

DESIRE + THOUGHT + EMOTION =
PHYSICAL OUTCOME

Let's explore how to harness the power of thought.

Understanding the Power of Thought

In essence, the power of thought is a Universal concept. When you read the description of the power of thought, understand that all people: Christian, Jewish, Muslim, Buddhist; male, female; adult, child, are identical in this sense. We were all born with the power to use our minds (albeit not in identical ways), and we have the freedom to discern how we want to use it. We also have the ability to control our thoughts by accepting the ones that will serve us and rejecting those that don't. We do this by standing back and observing, then making conscious decisions about what thoughts we want to own and which ones we want to release. Remember, we are all made of energy. Our outcomes depend on our use of this energy and on the faith that we are constantly manifesting the outcomes we desire.

How We Use It Shapes Our World

To make the power of thought easy to understand for everyone, we will start with an example. Take a moment and look around you. Maybe you are sitting on a chair or have a table next to you. You are surrounded by the walls of your office or your home. Most likely you have clothing on. You are holding this book (either physically or through some technology). Now, take a step back and allow yourself to understand how these things around you came about.

The first step to the creation of any man-made product is an idea. From that idea, the person made a plan. They needed to select the material from which the object needed to be made. They required manufacturers and vendors to assist them. They also needed to have the product assembled. Finally, they needed to create a marketing and sales strategy to get the finished product into consumers' hands. All these steps had to take place before you sat down, got dressed, or picked up this book, BUT all of these steps stem from one thing—an idea.

Now, imagine a different way this scenario may have worked out. To make it simple, let's use the chair as an example. Here, the same person had the idea—"I want to make a chair." Instead of sitting down and starting the plan to build the chair, manufacture it, and sell it, a different internal dialogue takes place. The person thinks. "Who am I to think I can make this chair?"

"I have never been that great at designing chairs, no one will want to buy them."

"I remember when Bob tried to start a chair company and he failed. I will surely fail." As you can imagine, the chair you are now sitting in would not exist. This is the power of thought. The only difference between these scenarios is how the thinker harnessed their power of thought. Remember, you are always the "thinker" in your own life.

Now that you know this, you are probably wondering, "How do I stop myself from thinking self-sabotaging thoughts?" The answer is you must train your mind. Can you imagine if your mind was trained to think only thoughts that would create an amazing world for you? Full of your dreams, desires, and filled with great intentions? What a world we would live in!

Here is one example of how you can change your thoughts:

First, you must identify your current thoughts and beliefs. Many people go through life on "auto-pilot;" waking up each morning, pouring their coffee, heading to work, heading home, and going to bed. The next day they wake up to do the exact same thing again without questioning, though they may feel some emptiness along the way. If you are not actively engaged in analyzing your beliefs and thoughts, you may not be aware of how they are affecting your outcomes.

Start here: For one week carry a note pad and jot down things you hear your inner voice saying each day. Pay special attention to the negative dialogue you have with yourself.

Write each and every notable thought down. At the end of the week, review the notepad and try to extract common themes or recurring thoughts. Chances are the things you see repeating are more than just regular every day thoughts. They are your beliefs.

Next, imagine what the life you want would look like if you could have it right now. Ask yourself whether or not your daily thoughts are getting you closer to or further from that picture. If they are getting you further away, determine what you have to believe about yourself and your life to have what you want. Take a moment to write these things down.

Remember, our thoughts are very similar to our habits. We have a tendency to make them reoccur over and over again, even when we are not consciously aware of this. Habits can be broken. Some easier than others, but all habits are possible to break. Changing these habitual thoughts takes repetition, persistence, and desire. Once you have harnessed the power of thought, you will regain control of your outcomes. You will begin to feel empowered as you realize that the seeds you are planting for your future are positive and abundant. Shift your energy, eLIVate your life.

LOVE

"When we love, we always strive to become better than we are. When we strive to become better than we are, everything around us becomes better too."
— Paulo Coelho, The Alchemist

"Love one another and help others to rise to the higher levels, simply by pouring out love. Love is infectious and the greatest healing energy."
—Sai Baba

Where is the Love?

How would you like to live in a world where you feel loved, appreciated, and grateful? You can. At this very moment, you have all the tools you need to feel loved, appreciated, and grateful every day.

Love is a very powerful word with many different meanings. We believe it means to share your unique gifts with others to help them love themselves and embrace their lives. Love must be practiced in everyday life—at work, at church, at home, or when interacting with strangers. Leading with love is a lifetime commitment that reminds us that we are all connected and can help each other.

Leading with love means you allow love to become the intention behind each of your actions. When a situation occurs in your life, you have a choice regarding how you will respond to it. You can choose to respond with anger, frustration, fear, or sadness; or you can choose to respond with love. This "love" response can change depending on the situation or the person you are responding to, but you will intuitively know what response is and is not love in each particular circumstance. For example, sometimes the loving action is to walk away from a person and no longer be in their life. Other times, it means to rush to someone's side.

Love is not just a lifetime commitment, but a minute to minute practice. We face our ego every moment; it wants to be right, wants to feel good about itself, and perceive itself as better than others. This is not something we can get away from. This is something to be aware of each moment. When you identify with a negative thought, whether it's about you or someone else, it's coming from your ego. This is not your true self because your true self is pure love.

Love is powerful because, just like energy, it can and will affect your outcomes. Remember, every moment of every day what you are feeling and thinking emanate around you in your vibrational bubble. If you are constantly emanating love, you will constantly attract love. It will be effortless. If you want your spouse to love you, you must focus on loving that person. The first step must come from you. If you want your co-workers to love you, you must focus on loving those people. When you place love in your experience by deliberately choosing to experience it, you will be abundant of it at all times.

Love is a powerful emotion. It allows two people to come together without judgment and bond over a shared passion, a relationship, or the need for connection. However, sometimes we can all struggle with allowing love to lead us on our journey. We are prone to mistakes when our emotional choices aren't motivated by love. How do you make sure to choose love every time you choose an emotion?

Steps to Living a Loving Life

Here are our suggested steps to living a more loving life:

Love Yourself

Although this may sound cliché, it is absolutely necessary to mention. If you do not love yourself, you take the false and negative information people have fed you over your lifetime and live that information out through your daily outcomes. Research shows that between the ages of zero and seven we are unable to keep out or filter negative information. As a result, we end up internalizing negative experiences and believing negative things we are told about ourselves. Sometimes, we even carry that negativity with us long after the person who was originally responsible for that message has left our lives. If we do not take action to eliminate this negative conditioning, we will act upon those negative beliefs and they will affect our lives long term. To combat this negative programming, we must remember what it feels like to love ourselves unconditionally. Although it may be hard to recognize this now, you were born perfect and loved yourself fully at one time. Now, it is time to go back to that place.

Steps to Loving Yourself

1. Identify the Belief

First, ask yourself what you believe about yourself. For example, a negative belief may sound like "I am not pretty enough," "I am not smart enough," or "I am not good enough." Then, ask yourself if this belief is true and whether you can know it is true with 100% certainty. Ask yourself what your life would be like if you continued to believe that. Finally, what would your life be like if that belief no longer existed? Would you start a business? Would you go out and meet more people? Would you be in a fulfilled, loving relationship?

Another exercise that helps is tracing back the roots of the belief. Can you remember the first time you felt this way about yourself? For example, can you remember being a small child who felt like you were not good enough because you received a failing grade on a test? If you can go back to the first time you felt this way, can you remember who you were before that? Chances are, before you formed this negative belief about yourself, you were full of love, joy and Light. Reconnect with that part of yourself now. It is still in there. Our true essence of love, joy, and Light never leaves us. It is we who choose to leave it and we can revoke that choice at any moment.

2. Give Yourself a Point of Reference

If you think you are not good enough, you are speaking to yourself in a very generalized and negative manner. Ask yourself this question—good enough compared to what/

whom? Is it true that you are not good enough? Give yourself more detailed questions. Good enough in what? Compared to whom? Are there things you *are* good at? Soon, you will realize these statements are too general and do nothing, but stop you from loving yourself and thus attracting love in different areas of your life.

Once you pinpoint what you are measuring yourself against, you can then ask whether that measurement is healthy or beneficial. For example, it may not be healthy to compare yourself to a model on the cover of a magazine at the drug store. It may be healthy to admire a successful businessperson and want to emulate his or her outstanding qualities. Getting a point of reference puts things in perspective for you. No matter where you are and where you have been, you are loved, you are accepted, and you can be anything you want.

In addition to putting things in perspective, giving ourselves a point of reference may illuminate the fact that our unique gifts and talents are meant to be used in a different way. For example, if you are "not good enough" at a sport compared to someone else, maybe you are meant to express your loving energy through another medium. This could be through a different professional career, or even a different sport. The fact that your unique Light does not shine at full capacity in a certain activity does not mean you are worth any less, or that your Light is any less special. It only means that you are meant to shine your Light differently than someone else. Ask yourself what *you* are good at. Identify your strengths and capitalize on those. When you learn to appreciate yourself as a unique blueprint for expression and begin to honor your true purpose, you will begin to thrive. Remember, like a fingerprint or a snowflake, you are completely unique. There is no one else like you on this earth that has the exact same talents in the same combination. Embrace your Light. The world needs it.

3. Change Your Belief

We can appreciate that loving yourself is a process and it may not happen overnight. We also know that your belief system has been with you for a very long time. As discussed previously, our beliefs originate from things we have been taught and experiences we have had. This results in repetitive thoughts that shape our experience. These negative, limiting thoughts and beliefs take some time to "unlearn." However, the best time to start this journey is now.

You need to start by asking yourself what you want out of your life. Our lives on this earth are our most valuable asset. We get only one and it goes by so quickly. All of us share the desire to maximize our experience on earth, and we can do so from living from a place of purpose and love.

Therefore, when you ask yourself what you want from life, ask from a genuine place. Don't worry about what anyone else will think. This is your journey and your dream. Ask yourself what you have to believe about yourself to get that dream. Write that belief down and own it. The more you repeat those positive, loving thoughts, the more you will become those thoughts. Remember, beautiful and wonderful people come in all shapes and sizes. They are from all nationalities, religions, and races. They were made to be unique for a very specific reason and there is a special task they must perform in this life. You are one of those people.

Step 2: Love Others

Just as important as self-love is the idea that we must love other people. We have already talked about our thoughts and how they impact our lives. It follows that when we think thoughts of love toward others and our surroundings, we emanate from within and attract more love. Similarly, when we are jealous, bitter, or resentful of others, we put that energy into the Universe and should not expect anything different in return. Earlier, you learned how powerful emotions can be when combined with thoughts; therefore, it is extremely important to shift your focus on love. All of humanity is connected and we need to start acting that way.

Even if a person bothers you, take a moment to analyze his or her behavior. Often times, a behavior that presents itself in a manner that does not look like love is actually a cry for love. Imagine a child who is trying to get his or her mother's attention by acting out. Until they get some kind of attention, whether it be positive or negative, the acting out will continue. If this person does not learn a healthier and more productive way to feel significant in life, they may grow into adults that act out in the same way they have always behaved. This person is crying out for love. Taking a different perspective on the person's behavior can help you have compassion. When we have compassion for someone we can connect to their feelings and remember to love them, despite how they may be portraying themselves in that moment.

Even the worst of human behavior can be tied to the need for love and significance. Tony Robbins is famous for talking about the six human needs. One of these needs is significance. A great example Tony gives relates to violence. He says that when a person has nothing, the fastest way for them to satisfy the human need for significance is by acting violently. For example, when someone points a gun at your head, they become the most important person in the world at that moment. Your life depends on them. Do you think this person wants to be loved in this way? Probably not, but they may feel it is their only choice. As hard as this is, we must learn to love all human beings—even the violent ones. In times of desperation, their cries for love have taken on a violent facade.

If you haven't experienced physical violence, you may still have been emotionally harmed by someone in your life... perhaps a friend or family member. How you choose to heal from this experience is up to you. Will you choose to believe the person intentionally hurt you or will you choose to understand that the person was a human being who makes mistakes despite doing their best? Choosing the latter makes the burden a lot easier to carry. If you have been hurt, choosing love will begin the healing process.

Everyone has a story and a purpose for their life. You are never going to know it and understand it fully, even if you think you can. People act the way they do as a way of receiving love or protecting themselves. This applies to someone who has done something that seems unforgiveable—even this person has acted out of fear.

Instead of personalizing the incident, try to remove yourself from the situation. eLIVate yourself to a place where you can view the situation from a distance, as though you were observing two spirits colliding. The person didn't take this action because there was something wrong with you.

They were in a state of pain, misunderstanding, suffering, lack of love, or protection. When you make the decision to love and forgive the person who has done this to you, you are not saying what they did was right. You are freeing yourself of the energy the trauma carries with it. You are releasing the pain and suffering. You are choosing love.

Sometimes choosing love is hard to do. There were a lot of things that happened that Lani could have held on to. Having grown up with a drug and alcohol addicted family member, she could have held a grudge against this person or remained angry for her lost childhood. Lani could have blamed this person for her feeling of being behind in life, as she did not have the academic or emotional support she needed growing up. Instead, Lani chose to look at the situation through eyes of love. She wrote the following letter.

"It is hard to sit down and write this, as about ten years have passed and so much has happened over that time. However, this is not the time or place to discuss all of them. The purpose of this letter is to tell you everything you need to now, in case I do not have much time to tell you before you pass away.

In the past ten years, I have worked hard. I graduated college, got accepted to a Master's program at Pepperdine's Straus Institute, and graduated law school in the top 4% of my class. I have opened my own law practice, where I help couples divorce peacefully. I am not angry at you or bitter and I am not going to sit here and tell you that I accomplished these great things despite my difficult childhood. Instead, I believe that these great things happened because adversity was part of my life path. Hard things needed to happen for me to evolve into the person I am today ... a person who helps people.

I am not going to reiterate all of the terrible things that happened. You may not remember them all due to your struggles with drugs and alcohol. You may be in denial. That is all fine. The only reason I write this is to tell you that I don't hate you and I forgive you. Through my life, I have learned that forgiveness can be a one-way street. You can forgive when the other person has not apologized and has not acknowledged the wrong they have perpetrated against you. In this manner, I have forgiven you.

When I think about you, which I often do, I try to think of the good things. The way I remember you, you were beautiful and talented. You had many blessings in your life. I try not to imagine the way you might be now and what ten more years of substance abuse have done to your mind, body and spirit. Often, I just pray that you are "ok" and that G-d is watching over you. I hope that you are safe and keep yourself out of harm's way.

I can only imagine how much pain you are in. Trust me, this is not a conflict I have experienced without thinking of you. I know that every day you wake up alone, without your family. I know that your body bears the scars of childbirth, yet you have lost one child to death and the other two to your disease. I am aware that you drink and use drugs to forget. You are probably just trying to numb the pain ... stuff it down to a place that it won't find you again. I am sure that despite these efforts, the pain finds you again and again.

Every day of my life I have to live with the fact that you are in pain, and that you might die alone. Every day of my life I have to live with the fact that you are absent from my life and from some of my most monumental moments—my college and law school graduations, the grand opening of my law practice, etc. I also have to live with the fact that the day I get married you will not be there, nor will you be there to hold my babies when I give birth. I want you to know that I realize you can't be there because of your disease and I forgive you.

All I want for you is happiness. I do not want you to suffer. I will never forget the small glimpses of you and your real heart that I had the pleasure to know. I will always remember that it is the disease that took you from our family and me. I want you to know that despite all of the pain, I forgive you and I am whole. Please do not try to reach out to me. I wrote this to tell you what I felt you needed to know, not to open Pandora's Box. I hope that you find your way back to the Light."

Remember, when we choose love, the way it manifests may vary depending on the person and situation. Sometimes, it means you will love someone from a distance, which is what happened here. Whatever it means for you at this point in time, know it is the only way you can truly move forward. Since energy becomes matter, the pain you feel will be carried in your body until you release it. This can come in the form of illness or other unintended consequence. The only way to let it go is by choosing love. Our hope is that, through this letter, you can learn to forgive someone who has harmed you. Maybe it is time to write your own letter, even if you don't send it. In the end, we are all trying to find our way back to the Light.

Steps to Loving Others

Step 1: Forgiveness

Forgiveness is not an easy concept for humans. In fact, we are the only species on the planet that punishes others and ourselves for the same action more than once. This self-punishment and punishment toward others stays inside us and begins to feel heavy, eating away at us every day. Without letting go, we will never be free of our pain.

As silly as this sounds, dogs can teach us a lot about love and forgiveness. They always live in the moment. They are always willing to give love, even to strangers. They are always happy to see their families. Dogs forgive instantly, as the past moments are no longer significant to them.

Our past moments are significant because we choose for them to be. We can choose to let go. It is in our control. We must forgive ourselves first—for all past mistakes—and choose to move forward with a clean slate. We must actively engage in the process of forgiving others that have harmed us. Remember, they are just people too. They make mistakes—knowing or unknowing.

An example of this concept is found in a story about a prisoner of war. The man was trapped in a Nazi concentration camp. Every day, a Nazi soldier would come to his cell with a hand-full of worms. The soldier would force the prisoner to eat the worms every day. For this, the prisoner resented him.

The prisoner carried this resentment with him even long after he was released, until, finally, the prisoner chose to find and forgive the soldier. Unfortunately, the man learned the soldier had passed away. Unsure what to do next; he took a walk by the river. He decided to ask G-d to help him forgive the soldier. The man was startled when an image of the soldier appeared in the river. The prisoner asked, "Why did you torture me by feeding me worms every day? It was so painful. I don't understand."

The soldier replied, "They would not allow me to give you any food. It was the only way I could keep you alive." The prisoner was able to forgive the soldier.

What happened at the river was symbolic. The man did not actually need to know the soldier's reasons in order to forgive him. He chose that path on his own and was given what he needed spiritually in order to move on. This is the spirit of forgiveness. It does not have anything to do with the person who hurt you. It comes from within.

Step 2: Open Your Heart

Many of us walk around jaded by things that have happened in our past. We are afraid to love and we are afraid to get hurt again. Although we can appreciate our human desire to avoid this kind of pain, it is important to remember love is what keeps us alive. It is a prized gift we have been given. Each person on this earth is capable of loving and being loved. Have an open heart and don't deprive yourself of your right to give and receive love. The simple act of opening your heart will allow you to fully express the person you were meant to be and to heal others in the process.

Step 3: Love What You Have

Remember, everything in your current surroundings is the result of your desires, thoughts and emotions. Even if your surroundings do not reflect everything you want right now, you must still honor them and express your love and gratitude toward them. The more you express these feelings, the more of these feelings you will generate. This is one of the keys to abundance. You will attract more of what you think about. It's time to start thinking about how grateful you are.

A person who loses a limb in an accident has two choices: he or she can spend the rest of their life mourning the loss of that limb, or they can be grateful that they were able to survive. Only one of these decisions provides an opportunity to choose to love the life they have and live like they have never lived before.

Here is a short exercise to help you with this. In The Secret, they mention the concept of the "gratitude rock." This is an object you keep close to you and focus on a couple times a day. When you take the rock out of your pocket, or put it in your pocket, count your blessings. This is a way of reminding yourself to express love and gratitude every day. The more love and gratitude you express, the more you will attract.

You can replace the gratitude rock with any object. You can even choose to make a list of the things you are grateful for and that you love each night. The important thing is when you recite what is on your list or call out your blessings as you hold your rock; you experience the love and gratitude in that moment. Reach inside and call upon those feelings.

To make your own gratitude practice, start by choosing your "anchor" object. This can be a rock, a coin, or anything else you feel is portable enough to carry with you on a daily basis. Next, sit down with a piece of paper. Write down ten things you are grateful for. Maybe those things are your family, your friends, or your business. Then, close your eyes and think about each item you wrote down, one-by-one.

When you picture this person or thing in your mind's eye, focus on the feelings you have about this person or thing. Feel the gratitude you have for this person or thing with every fiber of your being. Then, picture that gratitude in a white Light above your head and bring the white Light down into the object in your hands. When you have covered the whole list, you can open your eyes and you will have successfully anchored your feeling of gratitude into your object. Now, anytime you feel your thoughts and feelings are drifting away from a place of gratitude, pick up that object. It will transport you to the place you need to be to get back on track.

Step 4: Embrace the Truth About Love

The constant battle between good and evil, or G-d and the Devil, exists in many different religions. People live in constant fear that if they sin they will go to Hell. Over the years, religion has separated humans from G-d with these philosophies. People have been taught that G-d answers some prayers and not others, and that they can only be joined with G-d when they die and hopefully make it to Heaven. People are taught that Heaven is this mystical, faraway place and there are several conditions that must be met before we can arrive there. In fact, we are given the choice to be close to G-d or the Universe at any given moment, just like we can choose to experience our life on earth as Heaven or Hell.

We don't intend to take a religious position in this book. We do want to remind you that you are never separated from G-d or the Universe. We are all created from the same energy, like a drop of water in the ocean. We are all made of love. We are not separated from this love energy (G-d) and our choice to partake in the Heaven experience is in our hands right now. There is no Hell, no Devil, and no fear. There is only love. Any expression otherwise is a cry for love.

The sooner we understand this, the sooner we will come together as a civilization and love each other. No matter who you are or where your journey has taken you, you will always have the chance to come back to love. This energy is all encompassing and it never leaves us. It is only us who can choose to leave it. If you have made this choice in the past, you can choose right now, in this very moment, to come back to love. It is waiting for you.

"Earth Touching" – an abridged poem by Thich Nhat Hanh

> *Here is the foot of a tree.*
> *Here is an empty, quiet place*
> *Sit in peace.*
> *Don't let your thoughts lift you up into the air.*
> *Sit so that you can really touch the Earth*
> *and be one with her.*
> *She will welcome you because love never says, "This is the last";*
> *because Earth is a loving mother.*
> *She will never stop waiting for you.*

Imagine a world where you are fully healed and love yourself completely. Making this choice now gets us closer to a world where we hold love and forgiveness as core values—a world where everyone loves and respects themselves and others. This is how, one person at a time, we can change our world.

Choosing Love

We all have moments where we can choose love or fear. For example, when you are presented with a new opportunity like starting a business, you can allow your passion to propel you forward. When you do this, even if you encounter obstacles, you make the highest choice regarding how you will overcome them. As a result, you will find that everything works itself out. Sometimes, in retrospect, you may not even remember how you made it through the challenge. You will only know that you are still standing. When you choose fear, however, you may be paralyzed and unable to act. Fear has the ability to hold even the strongest people back from evolution and achieving their goals.

When you choose love, the missing pieces fall into place. You can, at any moment, choose to love and forgive those around you no matter where you are. You can also choose to love a certain circumstance in your life, even if it presents itself as a challenge. Love the person who cut you off while driving. Love the person who hands you your coffee at the coffee shop.

There are two phrases that can make love and forgiveness easy to attain. Say "Thank you" to those you value, and "I forgive you" to those who frustrate and anger you. We forget how a quick "How you are doing?" can change a person's mood. You can treat someone lovingly when you open the door for them at the grocery store, or, on a bigger scale, when you forgive someone who's hurt you. These small actions will lead to a greater love for the world around you. Choose love, eLIVate your life.

INSPIRATION

"I no have education. I have inspiration. If I was educated, I would be a damn fool."

-Bob Marley

An Introduction to Inspiration

Every outstanding figure in history began their journey with inspiration. They didn't just wake up one day and create something that changed history because they felt a little motivated. They had a calling that was so loud and a feeling so strong it could not be ignored. They were left with no choice but to manifest their destiny into something great. These exceptional figures are no different from you. There are two reasons why they stand out. First, they listened to their inspiration. Second, they acted on it.

Inspiration is a thought that comes to you from your higher self. There's a reason this phenomenal idea is in your mind and no one else's. It came to you for a reason. It chose you to manifest it. Inspiration is just the beginning; what you make of it is up to you. Are you going to be fearful? Are you going to doubt your inspiration? Do you not believe in it or in yourself? Become silent and listen for your custom personalized message of inspiration and then run with it.

There are many inspiring moments for all of us in life—even if those moments are fleeting. Unfortunately, the more we clutter our minds with media, pop culture, limiting thoughts, and other distractions, the less receptive we are to hearing our own inner voices. Even when we do, we are often full of excuses about why our ideas won't work or why we aren't smart enough, wealthy enough or good enough to act on those ideas. To uncover our true potential, we need to listen to our true inner voices again. This has become increasingly more difficult for us, as our minds are constantly under attack by messages around us portrayed by the media, and sometimes even those close to us.

Despite all this, however, you can still become inspired. Can you remember a time when you had an "Aha!" moment, and felt the light bulb in your mind flash? Go back to that time now. See again what you saw, hear what you heard, and feel what you felt. You would like to be inspired like that again, wouldn't you?

As mentioned before, when a person is inspired it is a message coming from their highest self. When we act on that feeling, with complete faith we are on the right path, we achieve our dreams and inspire others to live a life of purpose. Inspiration must be honored and never ignored.

How to Recognize When You Are Inspired

Inspiration feels different for everyone, and we believe that it starts with finding your life's purpose. Take a moment to ask yourself why you are here. Why are you working where you are? Why are you in the relationship you are? Why is your life on this earth important to you? Why do you wake up in the morning? As adults, we often jump on the proverbial treadmill and run aimlessly. We exhaust ourselves running full speed, and sometimes we are just running in place! To avoid this feeling, you must look within and find your life's purpose. You are unique, with unique gifts and talents. It's time to find out why you are here.

Here is an exercise that will allow you to rediscover your inner voice. Remember that time you felt inspired? Maybe it was recently, when you felt excited to prepare a specific meal. Maybe it was this morning on the way to work when a song on the radio inspired you. Take a moment to go back to that moment now and write down five thoughts that come to your mind when you reconnect to those feelings. Can you think of another time you felt connected to that same type of inspiration? Is there a specific stimulus you can link to your inspiration?

For some people, there is a specific way they become inspired. For example, some people get inspired when they are out on a run and not focused on any one thing in particular. Others become inspired during conversations with other people. The way you become inspired is not important. What matters most is that you get the message.

If you lived your life full of inspiration and truly heard the messages from your higher self, your life would be more fulfilled. The whole point behind inspiration is that it comes from something bigger than us, from something we are all connected to. We are all connected to our source, like a water drop is connected to the ocean. These messages come to us to make us better, and as a result we will make the world a better place.

These are the same messages animals get that tell them how to survive. For example, this is how bees know to pollinate flowers, how birds know how to fly in formation, and how whales know how to come up for air. This very intelligence is what makes the world continue to turn in a perfect and deliberate way. Animals are always able to act on this intelligence, because they are not conditioned to ignore it and because they are not over-stimulated with distractions. In order to reconnect to our Light source, we must silence our minds to everything else so we hear it again.

What Happens When You Don't Follow Your Inspiration

If you don't follow your inspiration and your true purpose, you're not going to be happy. In fact, our emotions are one of the most powerful indications of whether or not we are living in alignment with the inspired and purposeful parts of our beings. True emotions show what our soul desires. For example, think about what you feel when you wake up in the morning and start your day. When your alarm goes off and you begin to think through the morning ahead, what are the visceral reactions in your body? Are you excited to get a jump-start on your day, thinking about all of the challenges and tasks you will tackle? Or do you have a sense of anxiety or dread? If you are upset, anxious, or dreading anything about your day, there is something out of alignment.

That's not to say that every day you live your passion will be perfect. Even if you run the business of your dreams, there still may be days that are more challenging than others. There may even be things about the business itself you don't fully enjoy. Think about it! Paying the bills isn't exactly the most riveting task! However, if you wake up day after day feeling upset, drained, anxious, or dreading the day, you know for sure something is wrong. You are out of balance because you are not listening to your inspiration. It may be so bad that you can't hear your inner voice of inspiration anymore.

If you dismiss inspiration too often, it will give up on trying to reach you. Every time you dismiss inspiration, the piece of the Light that is sent to you burns out. This creates a blockage of energy, preventing the Light from reaching you with its pieces of inspiration. The Light will attempt to bring the energy down through your body, feel the blockage, and leave you. The good news is if you choose to start to listen to your inner voice again, you can bring the messages of inspiration back. To do so, you must be open to carrying out your true purpose.

It is up to you to choose to act on that inspiration. The choice allows the energy to reach you. Your action is what makes things happen. Listen for inspiration, eLIVate your life.

VISION

"The only thing worse than being blind is having sight but no vision"

—Hellen Keller

An Introduction to Vision

Your vision is the picture of the desired outcome you hold in your mind regardless of what is going on around you. Once you have become inspired and have embraced that feeling, your vision naturally begins to form. The two are deeply connected. This vision can come in the form of a goal, an idea, or an intuitive feeling when watching another model where you want to be. When you are creating your vision, make it the picture of what your inspiration would look like once it has been manifested into physical form. When you hold this picture and focus on it, you will be continually drawing it nearer and nearer to your present moment.

Think back to when you were a teenager. Do you remember you or your friends putting posters up of cars you wanted to buy, people you wanted to date, and role models you wanted to be just like? As teenagers, we don't realize that surrounding ourselves with these images will impact our lives in dramatic ways. When looking at these images on our walls we were thinking of the day when we would be driving those cars, dating those types of people, finding love in those friends and family members around us, and becoming the role models for the generation behind us.

Once you embrace the vision without judging whether or not it is "realistic," the power of the Universe goes to work to bring your vision into your physical reality.

Do You Have a Vision for Your Life?

Your vision is one of your most valuable assets. It will take you from wanting to having. Once you have become inspired, you must create a vision of the realization of your idea. You must hold that vision in your mind and close to your heart. You must live that vision even when others do not understand or support you—it is your calling to create this vision in the world. You have to know what that vision will feel like, how you will act when you achieve that vision, and align yourself to manifest it.

This vision can be anything from material things, to a job you have been called to do, finding your soul mate, traveling the world, experiencing a new culture, or learning a new language. Nothing in this world is here to limit you. Whatever your purpose guides you to do and whatever you feel called to do, envision it in your mind and make that idea or purpose your vision. There are no small miracles when you follow your vision.

How Vision Works

When you become inspired to do something, it is because your highest self is motivating you to evolve. An analogy we really like relates to stone and a sculptor. When you are born, you are like a rough, natural piece of stone. You may be unshapely with rough edges, as you have not yet been refined by life's lessons and by following your truth. Just like a sculptor can turn a natural piece of stone into a beautiful and intricate sculpture, you will be shaped by the Universe into the best and most abundant version of yourself. To be shaped, you must follow the signals from the Light that come through your inspiration and are solidified through your vision.

When you have an inspiring thought, you have a certain energetic vibration around your being. Consider this your frequency. The person you will be when you reach the end result and achieve your vision has a different energetic vibration. This is because the process of achieving your vision will transform you. One of the things visualization will do for you is allow you to, in that moment, match the energetic vibration of the person you will be when you have reached the finish line. This is for a few reasons.

First, when you visualize something, your brain cannot tell whether you are having a vision, or whether the situation or thing you are visualizing is real. For example, when an athlete envisions shooting a basketball, the same parts of his brain are active as when he is actually shooting. Similarly, when someone who had a stroke and has lost use of his arm, visualizes using their arm, the same part of the brain responsible for the movement of that arm is active. This research is actually being used to help stroke victims recover.

The point is, visualizing the person you will be, when you have that vision and picturing your current-self in place of your vision-self allows your brain to be in that place. Your conscious mind will believe your vision is happening in that moment. Therefore, you will begin to emanate the energy of your desired result into your physical outcome.

The second thing to note about visualization is its ability to activate the part of your brain responsible for recognition. We call this the reticular cortex. From our earlier example, we talked about the "yellow car" experiment. If you went out and purchased a yellow Volkswagen, you would begin to notice every car on the road like yours. This is not because there are suddenly more yellow VW's around, but because you have brought that car into your awareness. During visualization, the same thing happens. When you visualize, your brain accepts that your vision is occurring and it will bring your desired outcome into your awareness. This will take shape in various signs and signals from the Light that will get you closer to the out-picturing of your vision in your physical reality. The very act of bringing your vision into your awareness will match your energetic vibration to the desired outcome. This sets the dial on your vibrational bubble to exactly where you want it to be, thereby drawing your vision into your physical world. Your vision will get you closer to the life you imagine. Choose to follow your vision now.

Steps to Creating a Vision

1. Ask yourself what the end picture would look like in a perfect world. This could be the perfect mate, career, or situation. There is no judgment here.

This is your journey and you must allow your own inspiration to be your compass.

2. Create a vision board. You can do this in many different ways. You can take a piece of poster board and cut out things from magazines that communicate your vision. You can put your vision online. It doesn't matter how you do it, you just have to take the first step to making it happen. Creating your vision board is the first step from taking the vision from your mind into the physical world around you.
3. Write your goals and affirmations. Some feel they are the same, but they are different things altogether. Goals are specifically communicated and measurable. Affirmations are positive statements that support your overall sense of well-being and mission. Affirmations are just as important as goals. Think about it this way—when you are inspired to achieve a goal, the attainment of your goal will help shape you into a better version of yourself. When you reach the level to which you aspire, you will have a raised energetic vibration. Just like the act of visualization as explained above, the purpose of your affirmation is to get you ready, energetically, to be the person you will be when your goal has been achieved. Below are some examples of goals and affirmations to get you started on your journey:

"It is May 1, 2015 and I weigh ____ pounds. I have _____% body weight. I work out at the gym 5 times per week." Note here, the goal is written specifically. When goals are vague, they are less effective. An example of a vague goal would be "I am in shape." The Universe does not know what you mean! Be specific.

"I am in the best shape of my life," or, "I am beautiful." While affirmations are more general, they are still necessary. While you are in the process of achieving your vision, you need to provide yourself with as much support as possible.

The best time to say these affirmations is right when you wake up, and again as you fall asleep. This is when your mind is most open and is the easiest to align yourself with the vision you are going to achieve.

You have two parts to your mind—your conscious and your subconscious. Your conscious mind is the part of you that possesses logical reasoning skills. It knows the difference between what is true and what is false, and can often have objections to things you are trying to achieve. Conversely, your subconscious mind does not know the difference between true and false. Instead, it takes your word for it and begins to carry out the task it is given without question. The key to reciting your affirmations in the late evening and early morning is that you are relaxed enough to bypass the "gate keeper," or conscious mind, and get your positive messages directly into your subconscious.

When you say your affirmations, make sure they are framed in the positive. Your brain doesn't understand the words "not," "can't," and "won't." Whatever you say after these words is what your brain and higher self will think you are trying to create for yourself. An example of this "I am not going to be fat anymore" or" I don't want to be fat." Here, because your brain is processing the positive only, it hears "I want to be fat." In other words, make sure you are affirming what you *do* want instead of what you *don't* want! To do this use affirmations like "I am healthy. I am fit. I am thin. I am strong."

Once you have created your vision, written your goals, and created your affirmations, you will notice a shift almost immediately. You will start to catch hints the Light gives you to get closer to your goal. This happens for two reasons. First, there are about two million bits of information around you each second. You cannot process each and every one of these bits consciously; your brain starts to filter the information for you. This filtering happens in an instant and once it occurs, you are left with about 126 bits of information. The information your brain chooses to take in is based on your vision. If you are focused on a goal, your brain will choose to take in information that supports the attainment of that goal. If you are focused on the barriers to your goal, those frustrations and barriers will show up. A perfect example of this is when you have lost something small like your keys or your phone. When you focus on the frustration of not finding the object or the frustration that you will be late, the item never appears. Instead, try stopping, taking a breath, and focusing on the object. Visualize that object in your mind free of the frustrations and barriers. Once you do this, you'll always find the thing you are looking for.

Second, we talked about your reticular cortex or the recognition center in your brain. Like we discussed, this part of your brain can be programmed to recognize the things you focus on. Remember the example above about purchasing a new car. You may not have noticed these cars beforehand. There aren't suddenly more of these cars on the road. Instead, you have programmed your brain to notice them. The same thing will happen when you set your sights on your vision. You will notice the things you need to do in order to achieve your vision. Once you do, it is your job to seize those things.

Once you have set your heart and mind on your vision, make the decision to not give up. You owe it to yourself to see this vision through until you have accomplished it. You only live once. There may be obstacles, though most come in the form of your own limiting beliefs. It is important to stay focused in the face of these obstacles. If you continue to focus on your vision in the face of a challenge, you will grow stronger and more capable of achieving your dream. Even the most famous and successful people have faced challenges and been turned down. They never gave up.

If there is something you want, take a moment and sit down with yourself. Ask yourself what it would feel like to sit in your dream home, your dream car, or the desk chair in the perfect office of your most desired job. Look around and focus on what you see, what you hear, and how you feel. Don't think about the reasons why you can't or don't have those things. Don't focus on the excuses that may be holding you back. This is your life and it can be lived based on how you choose to envision it. You can envision a world of limitless abundance or of limitless obstacles. Your story is for you to write and rewrite however you choose. Turn this page of your story and write something new for yourself through the vision of what you truly desire and always let the Light guide you. Your inner truth will never steer you wrong. Focus on your vision, eLIVate your life.

ALIGNMENT Part 1: Limiting Beliefs

"When you find that your life is out of alignment with your grandest idea of yourself, seek to change it."
Neale Donald Walsch

"The more convinced of the power of the word, the more power will the word have."
– Ernest Holmes

"What you focus on, you will feel"
Tony Robbins

An Introduction to Alignment

Have you ever wished you knew what your true path was? Where it is hiding from you? If you were to just turn down a corner would it be hiding in the alleyway? If we showed you the true path, would you take it? Would you listen to the compass asking you to follow it? What if you always wanted to be something or someone different, but excuses you have relied on stood in your way?

We have all heard examples of the person who takes a job in corporate America or at the family business instead of following their heart. These people end up stuck in a job where the passion has run dry. Yes, it could be a more stable way to live, and it may even be easier to ignore your inner truth. However, your joy and passion will continue to call out to you every day as you stare at those sparse cubicle walls, every time you sit through a meeting where nothing is resolved, and spreadsheets all seem to have the same information. The moment you stop ignoring your inner truth and give in to the joy that is within your path will be the day you know the feeling of being in full alignment.

One of our favorite examples of someone who lives in alignment is a street entertainer named Isaac Hou. When his parents named him Isaac, they dreamed he would be a famous scientist or engineer. Throughout his whole life, Isaac was steered in that direction, but always felt a sense of emptiness and frustration. In his spare time, Isaac focused on learning street performances. He mastered the cyr wheel, which is a large steel hoop used to perform acrobatic feats.

After years of living his passion behind the scenes, Isaac made a decision to pursue what truly made him happy. Although his parents did not stand behind him, Isaac knew he would never live a happy life unless he remained true to his highest self. Isaac once said, “It’s easier when you know the path and you know the goal, but sometimes you only suspect that something is there and you have to make the path to find out if it even exists.” This quote is the essence of following your purpose in the face of uncertainty. Sometimes you can’t see the path, you are only certain that you must take a chance. You, yourself, must build the bridge to fulfillment with bricks made from your own desire for truth.

Just like Isaac, your right choice, although not always easy, is the one your heart tells you will work out for the best. It is the choice where you say to yourself, "I'm going to do this and I am going to be successful." Sometimes the right decision is the one where you have a good feeling, but you may also have some uncertainty. In the face of those uncertainties, you must choose to have faith in the end result you have envisioned.

These situations are very delicate. Sometimes they are stressful and make you feel as though you are under pressure. The dangerous part occurs when you are asleep at the wheel—when you allow fear to put you on autopilot. You must make sure if you are faced with something that doesn't feel fully aligned, you have a moment of lucidity. This is a moment where you take a conscious step back and ask your inner self if you feel aligned with what is occurring. Without this, fear will guide you into the darkness and you may not even see where it is leading you.

The decision to follow your purpose does not just impact your destiny. Through living your purpose, you have the opportunity to change the lives of many people around you. Using Isaac as an example, we can see how someone living their purpose in excellence inspires others. This can motivate those who observe you to change their own lives. This is how we can all work together to create a shift in consciousness.

Sometimes these choices can be a little painful. Being in alignment is just part of your journey. Once you get there, you grab onto faith and you start to take those steps between where you are now and where you want to be. Just because you are doing the right thing, it doesn't mean it's comfortable. We can promise you, what you are running towards is bigger than how you may feel in temporary moments of discomfort. When you take a look at your alignment you realize it is not only the right decision, it is what you must do. The aligned decision will have a stronger hold on you than your pain and discomfort.

How Alignment Feels

We all have one area of our lives that runs smoothly, like clockwork. For example, it is possible that you are fully aligned in your career. Therefore, you get promoted and are able to hit all of the goals you have set for your professional life. This is because your conscious and unconscious minds are in full alignment with your highest self in that one area. When your thoughts are in alignment with your stated goal and higher purpose, you will find that things in your life happen with ease. There is no resistance.

When your thoughts are out of alignment with your stated goal, each step toward that goal will feel like you are walking up hill or in quicksand. You may take three steps forward and four steps back, becoming increasingly more frustrated that you have deviated from the path to your dream. You will always recognize these areas because they will continually cause you pain and discomfort. This unaligned area may show up over and over again in different situations, and even with different people. An example is a person who gets into one bad relationship after another. They may leave one bad relationship and enter a completely different relationship with a new person, only to find that the same problems are repeating once again.

Thankfully, it is possible to re-align yourself so every aspect of your life runs smoothly, like a stream flowing to an ocean. The important thing to know is that the choice is yours. You have the power to choose to align your thoughts and remove the resistance, or to choose to remain in a place where obstacles will always find their way into your path. You can do this by looking within to determine what areas are out of alignment and then put those pieces back into place. However, before you can, you must fully understand the alignment pyramid.

The Alignment Pyramid

We believe every person's life can be divided into four parts: spiritual (this can be any belief system), mental (your thoughts and convictions), emotional (how you feel), and physical (your surroundings). When you are in alignment with these areas, the outcome in your physical surroundings will be exactly as you intend them to be. This requires a high level of congruency between your values, your goals/desires, your beliefs, your thoughts and your actions.

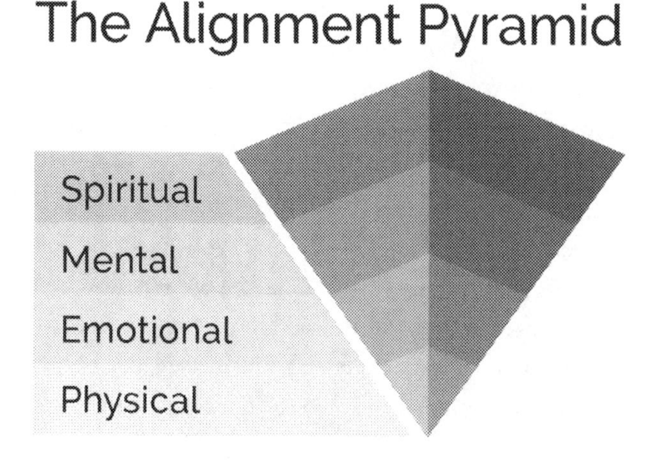

Getting in alignment starts with an understanding of what we call the "Alignment Pyramid." First, you must know who you are spiritually. You must have established your own personal connection to the Universe, G-d, or the higher power you believe in. If you do not believe in a higher power, then focus on your human connection to the Universe, as a creative and interconnected body of energy. This is also where your inspiration will come from. The inspiring thoughts and feelings are coming from your source with the intention of propelling you forward into your next personal phase of evolution.

The next step in the alignment pyramid, which is found below spirituality, is your mental state. Once you become in touch with your spiritual connection, you must form your own belief system. In other words, you must decide what you think about yourself, your relationship to the world around you, and what you are trying to accomplish. Just like Henry Ford said, "If you think you can, or you think you can't, you are right." This belief system should cover how you govern your own actions and thoughts, and how you relate to the world.

Your belief system is the map that is going to take you from where you are to where you are going. If you believe positive things about yourself and the world around you, you will attract good things into your experience. Conversely, if you believe negative things, you will attract negative people and experiences into your life. Once you have made this connection and identified your beliefs, you must focus your energy on the object of your desire. This could be anything that fulfills you; a business, a relationship, even a hobby or interest. You want this energy to form into thoughts, which you can then focus on creating in your experience. As you have already learned, your thoughts and beliefs are highly responsible for your outcomes. Therefore, you must ensure that your thoughts and beliefs are in alignment with who you are at your spiritual center.

Under your mental state, there is emotion. This is how you feel about certain things. It is perfectly healthy to experience and honor your emotions, but you must also be aware of how you assign meaning to things. You have emotions for a reason. They are an indicator that you are being faced with an opportunity to grow. When you are in pain, it can often be because you are being shaped into a stronger, better version of yourself. Emotions can also be an indication that we are out of alignment with a person or circumstance in our lives. Here, our emotions are a signal we must change our relationship to a person or situation.

However, emotions should not be given too much power. If they are allowed to rein over our lives, they can misguide us. Remember, our true state is that of happiness, abundance, and well-being. Anything that doesn't feel like that is a lesson being presented for our growth, and we must act on the lesson.

In order to observe your emotions in a meaningful way, try to observe a situation from an objective point of view and choose what it means to you. Imagine yourself as an outside observer watching the situation from afar. When you do this, you disassociate yourself from your emotions and observe the situation for what it really is. You are able to see your spirit interacting with the person or situation. At that point, you can determine whether that person or circumstance aligns with you or not. Then, you choose what it means. You are able to choose what meaning to assign to a certain situation. When you understand this, you also have the power to choose how you feel about things.

There is no such thing as a person who "makes" you feel a certain way. They are not forcing you to feel sad or angry. The person has acted on their own volition, and now you can choose what meaning to assign to an action and how you will feel about it. For example, if you get laid off from your job, you can choose for it to mean that your career is over. Conversely, you can choose for it to mean that you have a brand new opportunity to find a new and better job. Even in the face of a challenge, you must always do your best to place positive emotions on your desired outcomes.

Emotion is also important when you are in the process of manifesting a physical condition or a desired outcome into your experience. Remember, **desire + thoughts + emotion = physical outcome.** This is why it's really important for emotions to stay in alignment with your highest truth and thoughts about yourself and your environment. Alignment in the area of your emotions is often a challenge, not because it's a difficult process, but because it is a concept that most of us haven't practiced. For example, think about a time when something a person said upset you. You probably thought about it while driving home or another time you were alone. As you mentally replayed what was said, you may have begun feeling emotional about the conversation again. It was like the conversation was happening all over again even though the experience itself was over.

As you think and feel, the vibrations of energy from that emotion are emanating into the Universe and attracting more of what you feel. This is why you should allow yourself to experience and honor the emotions once, without allowing them to continually punish you. The level of emotion we allow ourselves to experience will, of course, vary depending on the circumstances. For example, if you are grieving the loss of a loved one, give yourself plenty of time. The emotions should be relative to the circumstances at hand.

Most of us go through moments like the ones described above on a regular basis, never questioning what we think and feel. As humans, we are the only species that continues to re-live experiences like this over and over again. While it can be beneficial to experience emotions relating to events, it can be harmful to keep repeating these emotions.

To practice alignment, we must analyze what we feel and do our best to put our thoughts and emotions back into alignment with our vision of our highest and best self. We do this by choosing to re-direct our focus from where we are now or the process that will need to occur for the end result to happen, to the feelings we will have when we attain the desired result. For example, you can envision a timeline. There is where you are right now, and where you want to be. What are you going to feel like when you are where you want to be? Those are the feelings you want to allow into your experience, as these are aligned with your vision from your highest self.

When we are out of alignment, it creates constant interference with our innate ability to attract what we want into our experience. For example, you may have a goal that you would like to lose 20 pounds. You have read about the law of attraction, so you sit down right away to create your vision board with all kinds of photos and images. You start out with the right energy behind it. Next, you write down affirmations. You read them every day. Now, let's say the emotion behind weight loss is fear. You have a deeply rooted fear of being overweight.

When fear is the deep emotion behind an outcome, it may serve to motivate you in the short term, but will not be positive in the long run. This is because fear is not in alignment with your higher spiritual self. You may have the right mental attitude. You may even exercise and maintain a healthy diet. However, as long as there is the emotion (often times hidden) of doubt or fear, you will not manifest the physical body that is 20 pounds lighter. In fact, you may find yourself doing things that are completely out of line with the end goal, like binge eating or constant cheat meals. Until you get your emotions into alignment with your true self, this will repeat like a broken record. This is an outward manifestation of the broken record playing in your subconscious mind. Remember, if something is out of alignment spiritually, mentally, or emotionally, it will be reflected in the circumstances of your life.

This brings us to physical part of the alignment pyramid. Envision a river trying to flow downstream. Without any dams or blockages in the river, the water is able to flow effortlessly downstream. This is how your life will feel when you are in alignment. However, if there is a block anywhere in your alignment pyramid, the physical outcomes you experience will not be congruent with what you desire. This is why we view physical outcomes in life as the symptomatic phase. In other words, your physical outcomes are actually symptoms of what is happening in your alignment pyramid.

Usually, when we have a symptom, our first instinct is to mask it. For example, if someone has a headache, they may take aspirin instead of considering the underlying root of the problem, which could be dehydration or too much stress. Similarly, if someone is short on money, they may take out a line of credit or open a credit card instead of examining their money mindset and taking a look at their alignment pyramid in that particular area. When there is a symptom in your life, or an undesirable physical outcome, you must look within instead of masking the situation with a quick fix. Ask yourself what you want and whether what you think and feel is getting you closer or farther away from that desired outcome. If it is the latter, you need to re-visit your alignment pyramid in that area of your life.

Walking Your Talk

In addition to the alignment pyramid, we associate another concept with alignment called "walking your talk." This means, if you are preaching health and wellness to others, you must have a clean and nutritious diet and exercise regularly. If you are a person who claims to be spiritual or religious, you must not only be kind to others while you are in church, but you must also practice kindness everywhere you are. This is the essence of being a congruent human being. You must live your values. You must be the example of your beliefs, values, and thoughts.

Alignment can be difficult to attain for some people and there are several explanations for this. Some people know the truth about their ability to control the circumstances in their lives and their ability to choose their reactions to things that they cannot control. However, they are not acting on this truth. Instead, they may walk around reciting messages they have read and remain in a constant state of unhappiness. We all have met the person who carries the self-help book around, but is constantly complaining about something. The thing holding people like this back is their own limiting beliefs. These are negative thoughts that create interference between your highest self, who is constantly striving to push you forward in life, and your physical world.

Limiting Beliefs

Limiting beliefs are thoughts about our environment or ourselves that are repeated so frequently they become part of our belief system. Once they become part of our belief system, they hold us back from achieving our dreams.

People are not born with limiting beliefs. We are all born knowing that we are creative beings of unlimited potential. This is 100% true, 100% of the time, for 100% of people. We are born determined, with an indomitable spirit. We are only born with two primal fears: the fear of falling and the fear of loud noises. These are survival instincts programmed into us at birth for our survival. These are fears that have been with us since our primitive ancestors walked the earth. Since we are not born with any other fears, their presence indicates our own limiting beliefs.

To demonstrate our innate and fearless nature, think of the baby learning to walk. The baby may fall thousands of times before the art of walking is learned and then mastered. No matter the number of falls, the baby's nature compels him or her to continue to get up and try again. There is never a thought that occurs in the baby's mind that says "maybe I am not good enough to learn to walk" or "trying to walk hurts too much" or "I could walk if only I had more resources."

If we are not born with them, then how do we pick up these negative belief patterns? Limiting beliefs can either come from things someone taught us, or learned from our past experiences, which shape how we see the world, and how we operate in relationship to it. Things we have been taught or that we have been through, created the paradigms within which we think about our capabilities, our relationships, our circumstances and ourselves. Specifically, fear and insecurity are states of mind that are learned and experienced, not things that we are born with. Unfortunately, fear and insecurity morph into things we believe about ourselves and the outside world that ultimately limit us; this is why we call them limiting beliefs.

More specifically, a limiting belief is defined as beliefs we have about ourselves or about the world that limits the way we live our life. Essentially, they are beliefs acting as filters of our reality. They don't just affect the way we see the world; they also affect the way we experience the world.

Limiting beliefs also affect our reality, as they contribute to how we assign meaning to things. This is because our perception shapes our reality. In fact, there are millions of bits of information around us at all times. The brain cannot absorb it all, so it begins to sort the information based on what it thinks is important to us. Our brain finds out what is most important to us by scanning our belief system database. Then, it filters out the information it deems to be useless.

For example, if we believe that the economy is bad, we will tend to absorb a lot more information to support this than if we believed that the economy was on the upswing. Since we can only perceive the information we are taking in and processing, this filtered information becomes our reality. In other words, our beliefs are always trying to prove themselves out for reinforcement and they will do so by manifesting outcomes in our experience and finding supporting information.

To counteract negative experiences, we have to choose a different meaning for things and change the lens through which we perceive them. Every time a situation happens, you have the power to choose, in that very moment, what it means to you. This is true of tragedy and triumph. You can make a tragedy into a lesson that helps you and those around you, or you can choose to allow it to mean that your life is ruined. This is a choice. We assign the meaning, as well as what we believe is learned. Therefore, it can be unlearned and replaced with new thoughts and habits.

Think back to the small child you once were. Those two things you were afraid of are the only things to fear in this life. Why do you have other fears and limiting beliefs now that you are an adult? There is a scientific explanation for this. When we evolved in our primitive stages, our amygdala developed. The amygdala is an almond shaped part of our brain responsible for observing and assessing situations we are confronted with and alerting us to potential danger. This part of the brain bases its assessment of danger by scanning our memory banks for previous or similar experiences. This is important, and will be discussed in more detail later on, as it relates to how this can hold us back.

However, over time and due to the changing nature of survival in modern times, the amygdala has evolved to become more sensitive, which is not always a good thing. This part of our brain has evolved to include a wide range of inputs such as love, hate, anger, fear, panic, and anxiety. Unfortunately due to this evolution, we are now wired to measure current situations and circumstances against past experiences and things we have been "taught" about our own safety and well-being. This results in amygdala activation when it is not necessary for our own safety, or desirable for our own well-being. In contrast, our fear response that was originally intended to protect us is in fact harming us without our knowledge. In fact, this can result in the formation of "limiting beliefs" as discussed below.

How Do Limiting Beliefs Arise?

(1) Triggering Event (Amygdala)

Let's say you took an exam in college and you didn't sleep the night before. You thought about this before the test and felt tired. Then you failed the exam. As a result, you may have programmed yourself to think, "If I do not sleep before an exam, I will fail." Now, every time you take an exam without a good night sleep under your belt, your amygdala kicks in with worry, fear, and anxiety. You may think "I didn't sleep last night; therefore, I will fail." When your amygdala is activated, it shuts down the parts of the brain that are responsible for our logical thinking. Therefore, when we are scared, we do not have the ability to think clearly and logically. This is an example of how our amygdala holds us back.

Now this belief "I have not slept, therefore I will fail" is supported by strong emotion produced by your amygdala (fear), it is likely that this outcome will become true. It is important to understand if you fail, it is not because your assumption is true. In other words, it is not true that you will fail simply because you didn't sleep. Instead, you will fail because your limiting belief, supported by emotion and conviction, caused you to manifest that truth. Remember, your belief is finding supporting information to reinforce itself once again.

Now that you understand the basic concept of the triggering event, it is important to point out this goes much deeper. The formation of the limiting belief due to a past experience could also arise from a very painful experience that has caused you to indirectly form a limiting belief. These are the most dangerous forms of limiting beliefs because often we are not aware of what they are or how they arose in the first place and their roots can be very deep.

An example of this is a victim of trauma. Let's use an example that may be difficult to digest, but is easy to understand. Let's say a child is abused by her parent. Every time she gets less than an "A" on a test, she is hit. We won't get into the psychoanalysis of the parent in this hypothetical, because most likely there are some very deep-rooted issues we are not here to assess. We can analyze the impact that this may have on the rest of the child's life. This child may grow to believe, "If I do not perform perfectly, I will be punished." This child may also believe that terrible things will happen if she is not perfect in every way.

As the child goes through life, this limiting belief may not surface right away. However, let's imagine this person is now an adult working for a publication company. She is trying to meet a deadline and turns in a "less than perfect" project to make sure it is on time. She believes "my work was not perfect. I am going to get fired." The next morning, her boss calls her into his office to talk about the project. She immediately assumes she is going to get fired and she becomes defensive. Her boss lets her go. It is possible her boss did not intend to fire her when she walked in. The intended conversation could have been about any topic related to the project. However, she acted according to her belief "my work was not perfect, therefore I will be fired." As a result, she was fired.

As you can see, limiting beliefs are circular. You believe it is going to happen, it happens, and then your belief in that thing is further strengthened. In other words, if you believe something, it will manifest. This is true whether what you believe is positive or negative.

(2) Taught (Prestige Suggestion)

Past experiences are not the only reason for the creation of limiting beliefs. In addition, although the people close to us always mean well, it is possible they teach us these limiting beliefs. Our parents, close friends, and relatives are all human. Thus, although they want the best for us and are coming from a good place in being concerned for our safety, they sometimes impose their own ideals of limitation on us. Remember, when we are born, we are completely aligned. We only have two primal fears. Unfortunately, misaligned adults begin to shape our impressionable belief systems from a very young age.

Here is an example: Fred tried to start a business in his early twenties and the business did not succeed. Then he went to work for a corporation and became very successful. When Fred's son, Bob, came to him at the age of 22 and said he wanted to start a business, Fred said "you shouldn't start a business in your early 20's. It is impossible to succeed. You are better off going to work for a corporation, where you are guaranteed to be successful."

Even though Fred means well, his own limiting belief is now being imposed on Bob. As a result, Bob may develop the very same limiting belief "people who start their own businesses in their early 20's usually fail. It is safer to work for a corporation, where you are guaranteed success."

It is important to notice in this hypothetical, it is unlikely that Bob will go out and seek a second opinion, or start his own business if he has a deep, trusting relationship with his father that is based on admiration and respect. This is because of the power of prestige suggestion. When you look up to or respect a person, and they teach you a limiting belief, it is very likely that you will adopt that belief into your own personal belief paradigm. The same is true when they tell you something positive. This is because our conscious mind, the "gate keeper" will not feel the need to keep this information from a source it has deemed "trusted" out.

In the same hypothetical, if Bob had spoken to someone else prior to speaking to Fred who had the opposite experience, Bob may have formed a positive belief. In addition, Bob could have researched the top 100 successful business owners who started in their early 20's and would have found tons of examples. Remember, this information could change the filter through which we see the situation and therefore completely change the course of the believer's life. The point here is Bob was taught something that was true for Fred, and did not necessarily have to be true for Bob.

Another example is a mother who tells her son "close the window. If there is a draft, you will get a cold." Now every time there is a draft, the son gets a cold. This happens because her son believes it, even though there are thousands of people all over the world who are exposed to drafts daily with no cold symptoms as a result. Beliefs are so powerful they can actually cause a physiological response. This is because our subconscious mind, which is responsible for our health and preservation, controls our bodily functions. If these messages get to your subconscious, it will carry out what it is told.

How Do Limiting Beliefs Affect my Power to Achieve?

At this point, you are probably wondering, how do my beliefs about the world influence my outcomes? The answer to this is very simple and relates to a concept we are all familiar with—cause and effect. Put simply, every thought is a cause and every condition is an effect. Emerson said, "A man is what he thinks about all day long." What he meant is that a man creates his own life based on his thoughts. The more frequent and repetitious the thoughts, the more power they have on your physical outcomes.

Here are some things to think about. You have probably heard people refer to the law of attraction. This concept has been brought to the mainstream by The Secret and other self-help authors who claim your thoughts attract the things you desire into your life. There is a lot of public criticism of this concept, as some people have tried the methods with no success. There are several factors that contribute to this and we would like to explain exactly what it takes to get these principles to work.

Before we give you a breakdown of why we think the techniques fail the user, we must re-enforce the fact that it is not because the law behind these methods does not work. The law is always working perfectly. It is like gravity, if you pick something up and then drop it, it will fall to the ground. The law is universal and applies to everyone and everything alike. Similarly, when you use the Law of Attraction correctly you will attract what you want. When you use it as an unaligned person, you will attract what you don't want. This will be true every single time for every single person.

The unfortunate part is that there is a circular nature to this law. If you don't believe it will work, or you focus on what you don't want, it will only create that outcome. To state it another way, if you say "this law won't work for me" and it doesn't, the law is working perfectly. Unfortunately, you have just reinforced your belief that the law doesn't work. Also if you focus on what you don't want and you get it, your belief that the law doesn't work for you may be reinforced. To break this circular pattern, you must learn why it happens. The best way to demonstrate this is through a very common example—money.

Your Hidden "Money Mindset"

Wealth and financial abundance is something that almost everyone strives for. However, only 2% of the United

States' population has the level of abundance considered independent wealth. Although the definition of wealth is different for everyone, we can all agree that the end goal is some level of financial freedom. What is holding the other 98% back? It is their limiting beliefs that relate directly to money.

Your relationship with your money is like any other relationship in your life, and the Law of Attraction applies to this relationship the same way. If you work on this relationship daily, give it its due attention, and cultivate a strong and healthy bond with it, it will flourish—and so will you. If you don't, or if you allow your "baggage" to enter the relationship, there will be a difficult road ahead. When we talk about baggage here we mean thoughts, beliefs, and emotions that are taking up space in your mind—harming you, instead of serving you. This directly relates to the alignment pyramid, which we discussed above. Not everyone has baggage to the same extent. Some carry a small briefcase and some carry multiple large suitcases.

Do you know how much baggage you personally carry? It can be dissected, organized, minimized, and eventually discarded. The baggage you carry ultimately manifests itself in the form of limiting beliefs, constantly holding you back from achieving your vision for success.

Just like any other limiting belief, the baggage that pertains to your relationship with money can also be taught or experienced. For example, you may have been taught "money doesn't grow on trees" or "all people who are rich are dishonest" or "you have to work until your back breaks for money." Conversely, you could have an experience that changes your relationship to money. If your parents filed bankruptcy and lost everything, you may start to believe that you can lose money in a heartbeat or that there is no such thing as financial security.

It is important to examine our own relationship with money. Our lives are centered on relationships, to other people and to aspects of ourselves—our money, our health, and our goals. As a result of these relationships, we all have our own hang-ups we need to deal with. We may have trust issues, boundary issues, or issues with intimacy. Learning to exist symbiotically with your money is no different. We still have those little hang-ups.

Often, what we struggle with is a distorted perception of money and what it means to really have wealth or success. Many don't realize that the ways they view money and wealth is the means by which they limit themselves to its growth. Essentially, there are certain limiting factors that for the reasons discussed—usually due to external factors affecting a person's reality—have deeply influenced that person's psyche in a way that inhibits true growth and understanding of their circumstances. These limiting factors are similar to fears that exist deep within each person. These fears, which we try to avoid, become the very thing that defines our reality (what we feared most has come upon us). In order to achieve the financial success you deserve, you need to shed the disempowering relationship that you have with money. This will allow you to use the Law of Attraction in a way that harmonizes your life. Convalescing this relationship is a journey of personal development, as well as a journey to ultimately achieve your vision for financial freedom.

What do abundance and success mean to you? You must define this yourself and decide what your core values are in life. When you become cognizant of what really matters to you beyond the scope of your day-to-day business deals and beyond the scope of your wealth, you are most aptly equipped to define the rate at which you will be successful. For some, it's the ability to travel and experience the world; for some it's being able to take care of their aging parents. For some it's being able to give their children everything they need to have healthy and successful lives. For others, it's the ability to have nice things, live healthy and happy lifestyles. Whatever your values, it's very important to be so aware of them that you can recite them as easily, and with as much consistency and accuracy, as you could recite the alphabet. This will put a more earthly and attainable grasp on your ultimate successes and will help you overcome any limiting factors inhibiting your growth.

Types of Limiting Beliefs Surrounding Money

Fearful, Frugal

This is the perpetual saver; a person who never spends money because he or she believes money will not come back. This is a very common fear, but will ultimately produce the reality they're trying to avoid. A frugal lifestyle may be ingrained in you from a very young age—perhaps by your parents, or because you grew up hearing or reading from authority figures, politicians, talk show hosts, and cable news syndicates stating it was the proper way to behave with your money. Whatever the external factor you may believe brought about this mentality, you have adopted it as your own.

Since you may have been taught it is wise and respectable to be frugal, you must be wondering what is wrong with this mentality. It is directly caused by a lack of financial growth. We all know it's smart to save money. For many there is a point at which this mentality becomes your overall reality. You can tell this is the case when the concept of saving money is constantly on your mind. This becomes a problem when the belief that you will never have enough money and you'll always need to save in order to someday achieve financial security becomes rooted in your psyche. This is the point when your constant belief that saving money will bring stability begins to limit you, and ultimately prevents the financial security you are looking for. The underlying belief is, "If I spend money, it will not return to me," when the belief should be, "When I spend money, it returns as an avalanche of abundance." Instead of viewing money as gone forever, view it as a boomerang that comes back paying dividends. This is within reason. You still need to be smart with your money, but there is a balance.

An example of the frugal-fear mindset is as follows: Mona, who grew up with 6 siblings, always had to share things. Her family was poor, but never hungry. She was under the impression she had to save because there was never enough to go around. She saw her dad work extremely hard to save every penny he could. This was the way he provided for his family. Both her parents were savers, so the kids would pass on clothes to one another to save money, and Mona's mother would do anything to save money. Mona was tired of the lifestyle of having to share and not having enough. She decided at a young age to work hard and save. Her money philosophy became anchored in the idea of saving money. Now, she is over 50 years old and she has not let go of the belief that she must save every penny she earns. She makes more than enough to be comfortable and live in luxury, to buy nice things, and allow herself to indulge. However, she chooses to be frugal about every purchase she makes. She will drive far to get the cheapest gas, she will sacrifice her convenience, her mental peace, and comfort—all to save money.

In business, the old – and seemingly counter-intuitive — mantra is that you need to spend money to make money. Any entrepreneur who's cultivated a business from the ground up can agree with this. This is the very same idea. You need to believe that you have the power to spend your own money how you wish in order to achieve your financial success.

Fear of Gain and Loss

Another extremely common mindset very similar to the frugality mentality is that having money means you could easily lose it. This relationship translates to a feeling of constant instability and is completely counter-productive to financial growth and progress.

Joe started a wildly successful business that took off almost effortlessly. Due to his success, he could easily take care of his parents and had the lifestyle he had always wanted for them and for himself. Eventually his story took a turn for the worst. After hearing of Joe's success, an old friend solicited him to invest in his startup. The investment seemed sound, and he felt proud to be in a place where he could financially help out a friend. After the transaction, the friend disappeared leaving in his wake a trail of questions and instability—not to mention taking a hearty portion of his wealth. When the investment inevitably tanked, it took Joe's confidence in his financial stability with it, despite all of the growth and success he had already achieved.

The important thing to realize is it wasn't the loss of the investment itself that caused Joe to change his perspective regarding financial stability and sustainability. Joe could have taken this experience as a lesson about doing his due diligence prior to investing, or could have just chalked it up as a non-winning investment. Investing can often be risky, and typically the person investing is aware of the risk and thick skinned enough to sustain it. Instead, Joe chose for this experience to mean, "If I take risks with my money by investing, I will lose everything." As a result, he began to believe that money can be taken away from you at any moment.

This type of belief about money is actually very common. It takes a little bit of tough love to overcome, but it can be done. Often times the people that have this mentality are playing the victim. They are constantly attributing their success to external factors, instead of their own mindset and actions. Just like some people feel like bad things happen *to* them, some people also believe that good things, like financial success, happen *to* them. It is the same belief—my outcomes are beyond my control.

Long term, sustainable personal success means taking 100% of the responsibility 100% of the time. Taking control of your financial security means taking ownership of your personal success—good or bad. When you take responsibility for your outcomes and set your mind to succeed regardless of external circumstances, you will be unaffected by the economy, seasons, and ups and downs.

To achieve this, you have to start by adopting a no-excuse attitude—one that takes full responsibility for everything that happens to your business or your finances. If you constantly believe that external factors out of your control will be the deciding factor in your financial success, then you will be right and you will ultimately eliminate yourself as one of those factors. On the other hand, if you accept full responsibility for what happens in your finances and your business, not taking into account any external properties, then you will find the success you achieve will be completely up to you, and practically effortless.

Money Doesn't Grow on Trees

Another limiting belief that can affect your financial well-being is, "I have to work hard for money." When you were growing up, maybe you were taught, "Money doesn't grow on trees." Maybe you only got your allowance after performing hours of back-breaking chores. We aren't against building a strong foundation for a healthy work ethic. We work very hard ourselves, but our belief is that money flows to us easily and freely. The "work" portion of it flows from doing what it takes to carry out our purpose. When you are passionate about what you do, it never feels like work. In fact, the work feels like it is being done through you, rather than being done by you. The feeling is amazing. Money becomes a side effect of living out your purpose and doing what you absolutely love. When you have this belief, it never feels like you have to break your back to make money.

For many, living with a healthy money mentality is a no-brainer—money comes and goes, but they will always know how to make it, lose some of it, and get it all back and more. Why do some people feel they must work their fingers to the bone in order to have any semblance of success? Many people identify too much with their financial belief system. When we think back to the American dream as it was originally conceived, we can all remember this country was founded on the principles of hard work and the promise of success in return. We can all recall images of people digging for gold, families traveling across America in horse drawn wagons, and men performing countless hours of manual labor on the railroad system. In a way, our country has been built on the idea that blood, sweat, and tears are the only way to get rewarded.

As a result, people feel that in order to have financial success, there is rarely time for a personal life outside of work. For them, it is always about working hard and not working smart. The definition of the pursuit of happiness begins to take shape in long days filled with hard work, and stress starts to define your relationship with your finances—and for obvious reasons, will inhibit its growth.

This is just like the parent who smothers their child—the child's growth is ultimately inhibited, their creativity stifled. Maybe they will never really grow into the person they were meant to be. This is the relationship that is cultivated with your finances when you overwork yourself to achieve success. The underlying belief is you are not good enough to deserve money unless you break your back and work harder than everyone around you. This is what we call a conditional limiting belief. You won't feel good about yourself unless a condition is satisfied. We must learn to love ourselves unconditionally in order to combat this belief system.

Here is an example of how this conditional limiting belief plays out. Jasmine grew up watching both parents work hard for their money. Her mom was always proud to say that she'd been working since she was young. Her dad took two jobs at times to support his small family. She adopted the money philosophy that she had to work hard to make money and feel secure. She is successful at what she does, but has no time to enjoy her success. It's been engrained in her brain as long as she works hard, she will feel financially secure. She will be unsuccessful at enjoying her life because she is working 80-hour weeks only to keep financial stability. There is nothing wrong with hard work, but *balance is key.*

You need to eliminate the fear that money and success will never come to you easily. We challenge you to find ways to eliminate this notion impeding your growth. It may mean learning to let go of some of that control. You may need to learn how to properly delegate and prioritize. Ultimately, if you are living out your purpose on this earth, you will be so passionate about the work you do it will be enjoyable every day of your life. Money becomes a side effect of the joy you will naturally experience. You are successful when you do not have to be paid a dollar for what you do—you love it that much.

Wealthy People Are Evil

There is a particular wealth mindset that has been constantly over-expressed in pop culture, the media, many of our colleges, and from our business associates. It is the belief that wealthy people have either lost sight of morality, or they engage in immoral practices in order to accumulate their wealth. Some also say things like, "Wealthy people are pretentious," or, "He just got lucky." These thoughts are limitations or fears.

It's important to keep in mind you can achieve lasting financial success without compromising your morals or integrity. In fact, your new relationship with wealth and the journey you took to achieve it can help strengthen your integrity and resolve. Placing value in material things doesn't have to translate to a shallow sense of reality or a lack of spirituality. Everything revolves around your personal values. If what you value in life is seeing your children thrive, then you may place a high priority in spending extra money for college. Or, if you place a high value on your ability to travel and experience different places and cultures, you may want to put aside extra money to stay in a nice hotel and eat at authentic restaurants. These values do relate to money and your use of it, but they do not make you materialistic.

Each one of us has a unique spiritual identity. This is your relationship with G-d, the Universe, or something greater than yourself. You will relate to this in an individual manner, even though we are all connected to the same source. Through this connection, you will be inspired to live your individual purpose on this earth. When you align your thoughts (the mental component) and how you feel about yourself and the world around you (emotions) with this purpose, you will manifest this in your external circumstances (the physical component). The point of bringing up this discussion here is to illustrate that your spiritual purpose comes from the highest place possible (G-d/Universe) and is trying to come to life through you. A natural consequence of this is the thing you are working toward manifesting will show up in your physical circumstances. You are answering your highest calling and the physical outcome is a side effect.

When you follow your purpose, you are naturally doing what you love and the money will follow. Steve Jobs is a shining example of this principal. He had a calling to make something great, and he didn't give up until he created the perfect computer. The natural result: financial abundance beyond his wildest dreams. When he created the computer, he was focused on perfection, not money. Now, his invention has been a tool used to help educate and connect people all over the world. Oprah created a talk show to connect with people on a basic human level. She was focused on helping people's voices be heard. Money was the natural result of her efforts. There is nothing under-handed or evil about either one of these examples.

The over-arching point is there are always going to be different types of people in the world. There are some people who do dishonest things to acquire money. There are drug dealers, mafia members, and white collar criminals. However, there are far more counter examples of people who made money honestly and by following their passion. You are in the position to choose what you believe about how others acquired their money and how they have responded to receiving money. Money does not change people. It merely makes them more of what they already are. If they are generous, they will become more generous. If they are selfish, they will become more selfish. The truth is an evil man is just a rich evil man when he has money and a poor evil man when he doesn't.

If you deeply believe people who have money were dishonest in order to acquire it, or that they are immoral because they have it, you are preventing money from manifesting itself in your own experience. Your mind says "I don't want to be like that, so I don't want any money." Your subconscious mind, the willing servant, carries out these instructions without questioning the integrity of your belief. Therefore, you must change your belief about others that have money. You can choose to form the positive belief any way you want. You can say, "This man is successful, he must be passionate about what he does," or, "This man is successful, I am happy for him. His success is proof of all of the abundance available to us at all times." To sum this up, changing your mindset about others who have money is another opportunity to choose love.

Think of the world like a game show where the host fills a phone booth up with money. It flies everywhere and everyone has their chance to grab us much as possible. Remind yourself on a constant basis that money is available and is all around us. We live in such an abundant Universe. No one was born with the exact same desires you have. No one else was born to fulfill your exact purpose. When you do what you love, the money will come. Dishonesty will not be required.

Summing Up Your Money Mindset

Ultimately, our thoughts place emphasis on these limiting factors because they have been repeated for so long they become comforting to us. As discussed before, we are really only born with two innate fears: the fear of falling and fear of loud noises. The rest have been developed since childhood. This happens through the process of "domestication," through the meaning we choose to believe about an experience, or even through adopting someone else's. The bottom line is any belief you carry within about your finances will only be true in your case because you believe it to be true. If you want a different end result, change your beliefs.

You must also recognize growth only happens when we are out of our comfort zones. We can all relate to a time where we had a slightly uncomfortable feeling in the pit of our stomach that was compelling us to move forward. When you feel that, it is time to commit to your personal journey for growth—which is hard work. The beginning of your journey to financial growth and independence starts by adopting the money philosophy that wealth, and your values relating to wealth, are your responsibility and your choice. You can choose to spend your money on what you value most—your family, your friends, your community, third world countries, etc. Challenge yourself to entertain the thought that money comes to you easily, effortlessly, and right now. We are born perfect, with no lack or limitation. Any experience that does not present itself as abundance is a result of our perception. Change this perception now and watch the money follow as a natural consequence of your new mindset.

Money is only one example of people's misuse of the Law of Attraction. This misuse is universal and shows up in the lack and discomfort in many areas of our lives. In order to understand how to use this law properly, we must fully understand the barriers in our way.

Limiting beliefs are constantly running through our minds, blocking the inspiration of Light that is flowing around you. Every time these moments occur, the vibration of your body changes, pushing away the abundance that is flowing around you every second of the day. Your dreams, true path, and the love you have earned and deserve are looking to enter your life. Purging limiting beliefs is the first step to allowing abundance into your experience. The second is breaking down the barriers you have subconsciously created and using your new beliefs as bricks to build walls that shut out all negativity.

ALIGNMENT Part 2: Barriers to Abundance

Abundance has many meanings to many people. It could mean having wealth, restoring lost time with loved ones, or pursuing our passions. When we look to nature we see how plants have done many things to break barriers to abundance in their search for light. If needed, the plant will grow around a wall to continue reaching upward into the light. They have created roots that are strong and dig deep into the ground to find every source of water and nutrients to thrive. Other plants have created beautiful flowers to attract bees to help them create another generation of their species, ensuring their survival.

Until this point you have been chasing the Light, trying to find ways to find abundance in your life. Sometimes, all you need to do is stand within the Light, open up your whole body to it, and let it come to you. Allow your roots to grow and see the water rushing beneath your feet. When this happens your beautiful and unique flower will begin to blossom. Now let us walk you through how to break down the barriers you have spent a lifetime creating.

Barriers to Abundance

1. Resistance:

In many famous self-help books, the topic "resistance" is mentioned. For example, in Napoleon Hill's Think and Grow Rich he states the steps to success call for "no hard labor." In the book, The Power of Your Subconscious Mind by Joseph Murphy, Ph.D, D.D., he repeatedly states you cannot beat your subconscious mind into submission. The point here is when you are in alignment, resistance is gone forever.

Approaching your mind with new beliefs and expecting there to be no resistance is easier said than done. As discussed previously, our limiting beliefs can be deeply engrained by past experiences or teachings to which we have been subjected. For example, if you have been taught that wealthy people are greedy, and you suddenly start telling yourself "I am wealthy" through an affirmation, you will have automatic resistance. The belief you are trying to instill is not aligned with your pre-existing moral compass. Therefore, before you can believe you are wealthy, you must first change your belief about wealth. If your belief is deeply engrained in your subconscious, this may take some time.

What to do About Resistance

Research shows that your subconscious mind is most impressionable right before you go to bed and right after you wake up in the morning. Therefore, these are the times you must impress new beliefs on your subconscious. In the example above, if the end belief you want is "I am wealthy," but you currently believe all wealthy people are greedy, you must first change the limiting belief. It will be helpful to find a contrary example. This means to find a real life example that is the opposite of what you believe. Warren Buffett gave the majority of his fortune to the Bill & Melinda Gates Foundation. Instead of keeping his money and spending it, he gave 85% of it to charity! This shows a wealthy person was generous, not greedy.

Once you have a solid example that resonates with you, focus on it before bed and first thing in the morning. Tell yourself that wealthy people are generous until you begin to believe it. Once you do, you will have removed your resistance to the concept of wealth and it will be easier to impress that idea upon your own mind.

Once you have gotten over the first hurdle then use the same technique to create the new belief, "I am wealthy." Before you go to bed at night and first thing in the morning repeat this affirmation. For now, a simple "I am" affirmation will work. When you have practiced this, please refer to the "Goals and Affirmations" section of this book, where we will teach you how to create effective goals and affirmations in an easy step-by-step process.

Fear

Fear is one of the hot topics in this book, covered several times because it is common to everyone and is a powerful block when it is activated. As explained before, the part of our brain that is responsible for fear evolved to keep us alive. Unfortunately, this part of our brain has now over-evolved and is holding us back. In The Power of Your Subconscious Mind, the author states, "When your desires and imagination are in conflict, your imagination invariably gains the day." This means if what you want is in conflict with fear, the fear will win. He gives a very relevant example for this principal.

He says,

> *"If you were asked to walk a plank on the floor, you would do so without question. Now suppose the same plank were placed twenty feet up in the air between two walls, would you walk it? Your desire to walk would be counteracted by your imagination or fear of falling. Your dominant idea which would be the picture of falling would conquer. Your desire, will, or effort to walk on the plank would be reversed and the dominant idea of failure would be reinforced."*

This is exactly how fear works. Any time you are in the presence of fear, you will be crippled. It is not your fault, it is by evolutionary design. When the part of the brain responsible for fear is activated, you are not able to think logically. You are not able to rationalize walking the plank suspended in air, because your brain is inhibited from thinking "I have walked the same plank on the ground hundreds of times, there is no reason I cannot walk it now." Fortunately, this fear can be untrained.

If you were a firefighter, you may have had the same fear of fire that we all do. However, a firefighter has been trained to run through fire without fear. You can do the same and it is all in your mental conditioning.

Another example of how fear will manifest itself in your life is when you have had a traumatic experience. A horse stumbles on a stump and gets cut as a result. Now, every time the horse passes the stump, he shies away. As a result, the horse's owner removes the stump from the ground by tearing it out of the soil by the roots and filling the hole with new soil. Still every time the horse passes the place where the stump used to be, he still shies away. The stump is no longer real, but the horse still shies away from the memory of the stump. We are just like this.

Remember, we said that our amygdala measures safety of a situation against past experiences. If we have a past experience that renders something unsafe, even if the dangerous condition has been removed, we may still act as though it is there. In people, this often shows up in relationships. A man cheats on his wife with a woman he met at work. Years after their divorce, she is dating someone new. This man has no intention of cheating on the woman, but she is suspicious of everyone the new man works with. The dangerous condition, her ex-husband and his affair, has been removed. She is left with fear that any partner she meets will cheat with someone at his place of work. Her amygdala tells her, relationships are not safe and she acts accordingly. As a result, the operation of fear in her life is holding her back.

What to do About Fear

Step 1: Identify Your Fear and Face it

When we have a fear in our mind we fail to specifically identify and face, it seems bigger in our minds than it really is. Remember the stump example. Write down your specific fear(s) and try to understand them. Once you understand the fear, face it. You may want to literally face your fear. For example, if you are a salesperson and your fear is rejection, go knock on some doors and experience it. Create an affirmation that deals with this rejection and will allow you to dispel its negative effects.

This is the first step in the process of reconditioning. If your brain and body get used to this fear, they will get desensitized. Your brain needs to learn the difference between fear that is necessary to keep you alive and fear that will have no impact on your immediate survival. When your brain recognizes the fear is not necessary to keep you alive, you can re-condition yourself not to feel it.

Here is an exercise to identify your fear:

- Write out limiting beliefs about yourself. Between 20-100
- Ask if they are really true. If you think they are, can you know they are true with 100% certainty?
- When did you start believing this and why?
- Who would you be without this belief?

Step 2: Connect Your Intention to Action

First, ask yourself, "If I continued believing this, what would my life be like? If I continued to believe I am not good enough to be successful in business, what would my life be like?" Understanding the potential consequences of what you currently believe helps you see where you really are in relation to where you want to be. When doing this exercise, be very descriptive about what you believe the future would hold if you continued believing what you do right now.

Second, ask yourself, "What you would want your future to look like?" Just like the above exercise, you need to be specific about this mental picture. The details are very important, as they must be clearly communicated to your subconscious mind. Once you have done this, ask yourself, "What do I need to believe for my life to be like this?"

Third, once you have identified what the new belief must be, start building a bridge, one brick at a time, to your new life. You must have a strategy to take your life from where it is right now to where you want it to be. Start by making the new belief into specific goals and affirmations. Then you will need to act accordingly. Remember, fears are starved by action. Sometimes you need to jump in order to move through fear. When you start to move forward immediately, you reduce the time between imagination of the idea and action. This takes the power away from your fear.

Step 3: Thank Your Mind and Allow it to Release the Fear

As we mentioned earlier, one of the prime functions of your subconscious mind is to maintain and operate your body for optimal health. Therefore, your mind may be conditioned to believe that fear is necessary to protect you in certain circumstances when it really isn't. Here is an exercise for letting this go.

Script: Subconscious mind—thank you for giving me a signal. Does this situation require my immediate attention? Is there a lesson I am supposed to gain from this? Thank you for this lesson. You can release the fear now.

Step 4: Act Fast

The general idea is the faster you implement an idea, the less fear you will have. The less time you spend between the idea and the action itself, the more successful you will be. We call this the speed of implementation. This is important because a lot of hidden limiting beliefs can arise between the phase of an idea and the actions to execute that idea. This is where you have to be careful; limiting thoughts such as "I do not have enough information," or "I have not done enough schooling," or "I have not done enough planning," may kick up. There is an old Chinese proverb that says "The best time to plant a tree was 20 years ago. The second best time is now." Don't fall victim to paralysis by analysis. Get just enough information to move forward and course correct if necessary.

When you relate this idea to the topic of alignment, you realize that acting on our inspiration quickly is very important. This is because the higher the speed of implementation, the less time you have to think about why it doesn't work. In other words, you are ensuring your thoughts (the mental component of the alignment pyramid) are in line with your inspiration, which comes to you on a spiritual level. This shifts the odds in favor of the outcome manifesting itself in physical form.

When you have an idea that you are passionate about, there is a reason for it. The Universe wants you to evolve and create this thing, whether it is a business, relationship, or product. If you have the end goal in mind, the steps will unfold along the way. You just need to act. It is not beneficial to put your dreams on hold because you think you are not smart, educated, well planned, etc. The Universe has given you everything you need—right here, right now. Nothing eliminates anxiety faster than action!

Step 5: Take a Leap of Faith

This step ties into step 4. When you are passionate about an idea and start to visualize your future, you must have complete faith in the strength of your idea and your path, as well as your own fortitude. You must have so much faith that you are "all in." There can be no Plan B. We like to say, "Jump knowing that the net will appear."

There is a story about a general who takes his soldiers to war on foreign soil. They sailed to the shore of the enemy's territory and the general ordered his soldiers to burn the ship. This left them with two choices—dying on enemy soil, or returning home in captured ships. The result—victory. Leave yourself with no choice but success. This is the act of moving forward with full faith in your own success—it is the only option. When you do this, you allow all your energy to flow into the desired outcome.

On the other hand, when you just put your toe in the water to test the temperature, the act of moving forward with partial faith sets you up for failure. It means that you do not have enough faith you will succeed. Lack of faith is enough to cause you to fail. Remember, your belief system is the map that directs your actions and allows the Light to show you your path to greatness. If you have a half-hearted belief, your steps will be vague and uncertain.

The leap of faith is not to be confused with blind faith or an uneducated decision. If you are inspired, think about the idea first. If your thoughts are in alignment with the inspiration (mental) and you feel strongly and positively about your goal (emotional), then go after it with full force. Only full faith will produce the full (physical) result you desire.

3. Language

It is helpful to compare your subconscious mind to a computer. Imagine you want to find the answer to something. You log on to your computer and search a topic on the internet. If your search terms were relevant to what you were looking for, the answer will come up right away. However, if you are not specific enough, you may get too many answers, or even the wrong one. Your brain works just like this—bad in is bad out.

Your subconscious mind is so amazing it knows everything about you. As the part of your mind that controls all bodily functions, your subconscious mind has a blueprint of your physical body. This includes every blemish, every freckle, etc. If you say to yourself, "I am flawed," your subconscious mind will be able to give you millions of bits of information to support that belief. What you get depends on your search. If you say, "I am smart" your subconscious will bring up the information that responds to that entry. It is important to give your mind positive entries. This simple change alone enables people to focus on the positive, which causes negative circumstances or conditions to fade away automatically, without any additional effort.

Another part of this equation is the specificity of the language used. Just like typing a search term in order to get the desired answer, you must be very specific in the terms you give your subconscious mind. For example, someone may say, "I am in shape." Their mind does not know how to quantify the term "in shape" because there are no specific details. It would be more beneficial for the person to say, "I weigh (desired weight)," or, "I can run _______ miles." They need to define what the term "in shape" means to them so the subconscious can deliver on those instructions.

Another example, used by Dr. Bruce Lipton, compares your subconscious mind to the car manufacturing system. Before a car is manufactured, there is a blueprint in place. This blueprint contains every piece of information needed to build the car from the ground up. Every part, every screw, and every curve of the car has been mapped out in advance. Due to the use of blueprints, 99 percent of cars manufactured come out perfectly and can operate for years. Just like this, your subconscious mind has a perfect blueprint of optimal health for your body.

After the car is manufactured, its longevity and overall appearance depends on the owner of the vehicle. If the owner garages the car, services it regularly, and has it cleaned, it will last a lot longer than if the owner neglects the car and leaves it out in the sun all day. The car's life span depends entirely on the decisions of its owner. Just like this, we are born perfect and we are faced with many decisions. The first of such decisions is how we think. From this comes a multitude of different decisions like what we will eat, whether or not we exercise and stretch, how much we sleep, and if we take our vitamins.

Just like a car needs shelter, service, and fuel to live out its full potential, we must maintain our thoughts, diets, and environment. We have to keep our thoughts pure and choose positive meanings for our experiences. We must be grateful for the vessel we were given. Our beliefs must be aligned with what we want. This includes our beliefs about how much self-care we deserve and how we choose to live out each day.

Another example: You order something and schedule a delivery. You enter an office address without providing a suite number. The carrier of your package may get all the way to your building, and even enter the doors, but cannot deliver the package because they do not know the specific suite. Just like this, your subconscious may be trying to deliver your goals and dreams, but you have not given it specific enough instructions.

To get to your goals, there are two simple steps:

1. Define the goal specifically. For example, what does "in shape" or "financially independent" mean to you?

It does not matter what these things mean to anyone else. This is your life and your journey. Be honest with yourself about what you truly want. This is not about anyone else's expectations of you. It is about what it will take to make you feel happy and accomplished.

2. Make a specifically worded goal. Example "It is October 1, 2015 and I weigh 125 pounds. I am able to run three miles at a seven minute-per-mile pace."

Remember, your subconscious needs specific direction from you. If your instructions are vague, the package may be in the building and still not reach your doorstep. In addition, your mind will need the goal to be worded in terms of what you *do* want rather than what you don't want. This is because our mind does not process negatives. Have you ever heard a person say "don't think about the purple elephant in the room?" What is the first thing burned in your mind? A purple elephant! Similarly, if you say, "I don't want to be poor," or, "I don't want to be fat," your mind will hear "be poor" or "be fat." To avoid this, make sure to give your mind instructions about what you do want.

Another helpful tool is to identify why you are trying to accomplish the goal. As we mentioned before, your inspiration comes from the highest, most eLIVated level—your spiritual connection. It comes to you for a specific reason. For example, if you want to start a business, is it because you want to reach and help many people? Write down your personal "why" and add that to your goal. Here is an example of a completed goal statement: "It is October 1, 2015 and I weigh 130 pounds. I have normal blood pressure and I am healthy. Therefore, I will live a long life with my family by my side." Writing your goals in terms that your mind can understand and respond to will give you the greatest chance of success.

4. Failure to Act (Seize)

If you have done everything else right, but are still not seeing the results you want, it may be due to a failure to act. Sometimes, this is referred to as seizing. When you have created a vision and are focused on a goal, you do not usually have to think about the steps that will be required to get there. The Light does this part for you.

There are some exceptions, of course. For example, if you want to become a lawyer, you will need to complete college, take the LSAT examination, apply to law school, pass law school, and then pass the bar examination. This is logical. The important thing to learn here is that your brain is already structured in a way that will help you achieve your goals.

Let's go back to the example of when you have just purchased a brand new car—a white Honda Accord. Prior to your purchase, you may have noticed the vehicle on the road here and there, but now, you see every single one! Is it because there are more white Honda Accords on the road? No. It is because your brain is now set to filter information in a manner allowing you to recognize that car. You have programmed your reticular cortex to recognize your new car because you are focused on it.

Goal setting works the same way. Your brain will tune in, start to focus on a goal, and will actually show you all of the bits of information necessary to get you closer to that goal. The key is, you must be open to it and you have to pay attention. When you see those signs, you must act on them immediately. These are the stepping-stones to achievement. When people see these signs but fail to act, they do not get closer to their goals.

Here are some examples of failure to act:

- I have to have an MBA before I can advance in my career
- I have to work for someone else before I will know enough to start a business of my own

- I can't have the career I want because it is too competitive
- I don't have enough information to make a decision

Strategic speed is very important. Information is great to get you started and, as we mentioned before, it is necessary if your desired profession requires a specific skill set. We would never tell you to perform brain surgery without the proper education and experience. Strategic planning is important, but it is possible to do so much planning that you never get started. Information is power, but not if you feel that you need so much that it holds you back. You must realize that growth will always involve learning. You can't go into any business venture knowing exactly what will happen. You also can't start a new job and predict everything that will occur. You need to have enough information to act, and then continue to learn on your feet, course correcting where necessary. If your eyes are fixed firmly on the prize, your brain will continue to gather the information you need to succeed at whatever it is. This may come in the form of an article you stumble upon, a person you meet, or another experience. Just keep on paying attention to the signs.

Celebrity Examples of the Power of Thought in Action:

"Before I had it, I'd close my eyes and imagine." Kanye West

"You have to expect things of yourself before you can do them." Michael Jordan

"Started from the bottom now we're here." Drake

"Don't stop believing. Hold on to that feeling." Journey

"Living on a prayer." Bon Jovi

"I used to dream about the life I'm living now." Lil Wayne, Birdman and Jay Sean

"As soon as you make one step you visualize the next step." Taylor Swift

"The harder you work ... and visualize something, the luckier you get." Seal

"Everything I make as a producer, I visualize it as a DJ first." David Guetta

"I would visualize things coming to me. It would just make me feel better. Visualization works if you work hard." Jim Carrey

"When I was very young I visualized myself being and having what it was I wanted. Mentally I never had any doubts about it. The mind is really so incredible. Before I won my first Mr. Universe title, I walked around the tournament like I owned it. The title was already mine. I had won it so many times in my mind that there was no doubt I would win it. Then, when I moved on to the movies—the same thing. I visualized myself being a famous actor and earning big money. I could feel and taste success. I just knew it would all happen." Arnold Schwarzenegger

"I visualized where I wanted to be, what kind of player I wanted to become. I knew exactly where I wanted to go, and I focused on getting there." Michael Jordan

Beliefs

As we have previously discussed, your beliefs are like the map your mind uses to accomplish things. Your beliefs shape your outlook on life, they filter through which information is perceived and interpreted by your brain, and your actions.

If your beliefs are not aligned with your destination, you may never arrive. That is why it is very important to understand your beliefs and the way to uncover them is to monitor your thoughts.

Remember the notepad we asked you to write your thoughts in for a week to look for repeating themes? Once you have your thoughts on paper, you can directly trace them to your belief systems. This will be especially true if you are able to recognize patterns in your thinking. You may find yourself thinking, "I can't get a better job," or, "The job market is terrible and no one will pay me more for the type of work I do." You can trace this to a few different beliefs: (1) I am not good enough to get a better job. (2) I am not confident enough in myself to know I deserve a better job. (3) My fate depends on external circumstances (e.g. the economy). Once you have identified the beliefs, you can start to change them.

It is possible the same person can have very separate sets of belief systems as those beliefs pertain to different areas of their life. As you analyze your beliefs and the language you use to describe them to yourself, you will notice in certain aspects in your life you have positive, productive, uplifting beliefs, and you are already successful in that area. You may also be able to identify some negative, counter-productive beliefs. For example, you can have positive and uplifting beliefs when it comes to family and career, but when it comes to health, you believe you don't have time to work out, or you can't lose weight. The best thing to do is not to think of these beliefs in terms of their truth – meaning you should not care whether these beliefs are true or false from a factual standpoint. Instead, you must ask yourself whether the belief you have is useful to you or not. If, "I don't have time to exercise" gives you a constant excuse not to exercise, then the belief is not serving you and has to change. The thought must be replaced and the language needs to be eliminated immediately.

In addition to identifying the beliefs individually, you will start to see belief patterns illuminate. You may also discover you have some very strong beliefs that rise to the level of convictions. These are beliefs you would defend when they are questioned, regardless of who is doing the questioning. You have definitively accepted them as true, whether they can be objectively proven as true or not. When you come across a conviction, you must examine it in more detail than other beliefs. These convictions are directing your circumstances more than any of your other beliefs.

Distractions

In our rapidly growing modern society, our days are flooded with distractions. We wake up to an alarm clock, read the news, watch television, check Facebook, and submerge ourselves in pop culture every chance we get. Unfortunately, it doesn't end here. Pop culture has become a method of communicating with one another, as we begin to assimilate the language from what we watch, read, and listen to into our daily interactions with others. The topics we watch on the news, regular television programming, and read about on social media become the topics of our in-person conversations. We are spending so much time immersed in this virtual culture that we are no longer able to connect with one another otherwise. We are not formulating our own thoughts or taking the time to look inside. This is crucial. If you add up the hours you spend engaging in these distracting behaviors, we guarantee there would be a lot more time in your days, weeks, months and years to accomplish your dreams. It's doubtful that Albert Einstein was reading about the Brittany Spears' of his day.

The News

It is worth repeating: a life of distraction is not a life of significance. Immersing yourself in watching and reading the news doesn't start your day on a positive note. If you are not able to do something about the problem immediately, with your own two hands, why spend time talking about the problems? These negative messages get into the minds of the masses, which starts their days with negativity and continues to spread it to their peers from the moment they arrive at work. Information about the "downfall of the economy," violence and other sad disturbing messages echo from our televisions and newspapers into our cars, phones, and offices. We are doing nothing but spreading the negativity even more.

It sounds crazy; we are telling you to ignore the news. Every time we discuss this with people, they push back and tell us that they want to stay informed of current events and remain "in the know." They choose to spend their energy filling their minds with negative current events they are not actively doing anything to change. There are miracles that occur every single day in this country and around the world. The media just chooses not to highlight these every day miracles for us. As a result, our society wakes up and focuses on the negative instead of the positive every day.

Don Henley, in his 1982 hit "Dirty Laundry" said it best:

> *"People love it when you lose. They love dirty laundry ... got the bubble headed bleached blonde, comes on at five. She can tell you about the plane crash with a gleam in her eye. It's interesting when people die. Give us dirty laundry."*

This is the essence of modern media.

You choose how you start your day. You don't have to start it with negative stories chosen by the media. Instead of waking up and reading the news on your smart phone or in the newspaper, try writing down your affirmations, or reviewing them in the morning instead. You will immediately feel that you started your day in a more positive direction. If you are the type of person trying to initiate change in the world, spend the time you would have used to read or watch the news doing a project for charity. Doing a good deed is more productive than reading about problems.

Pop Culture

While many people are caught up in their daily cycle of waking up to go to a job they dislike, they come home to watch their favorite television show at night. The viewer begins to look into the lives of the people depicted in reality television and believes this is how "real life" should be. They begin to engage with the drama, feeling the emotions, experiencing the ups and downs, and sharing the stories with their own friends and families. At the same time, they compare themselves to the actors, wishing they looked like them or shared in their lifestyle. This does nothing but bring the viewer down. The next day, the drama is relived every time it's brought up in conversation. This takes away our need to converse with each other about our own lives, hopes, and dreams. We no longer have to think up topics of conversation. In a sense, this makes us less creative, less independent, and less unique.

To try to break the habit, try to spend an hour each evening meditating or reading a book instead of watching television. See if you wake up feeling more relaxed and more motivated. You might feel less motivated to gossip when you get to work the next day. This will give you an added opportunity to go within and explore who you really are. You can rekindle your connection to your highest self.

There is an old story about two gods having a conversation about where to hide happiness from man. The first god said, "Hide it on the top of a mountain, he will never find it."

The second god responded saying, "No, man will eventually climb that mountain and find happiness."

The first god said, "Why not at the bottom of the ocean? Man will surely not look there for happiness."

The second god responded saying, "No, man will eventually dive to the bottom of the ocean and discover happiness there."

Finally, the second god suggested, "Hide happiness inside of man because man would never look there!"

With all of the distractions around us, this has become true. The truth is you were born with the ability to find happiness anytime, anywhere, no matter what is happening in your life, in the news, or in the world. It has always been inside of you.

Social Media

Today's generation is unique. We are the first to be so interconnected that with the click of a button, we see what people are doing at any moment. Social media has become a way for us to reconnect with people we have lost touch with and a way to keep up with current events in the lives of our friends. What is the problem? Let's start here. How many people do you personally know that check Facebook, Twitter, or Instagram more than one time a day? Are you one of these people? What productive action could you take more often if you were not engaged in social media? Are the people you are "friends" with on these platforms actually a friend? If you had a real problem or an important event to share with someone, would you call all of them?

You may be spending too much time finding out what other people are doing. To be successful, sometimes you have to look up from your device and focus on what you are doing in the current moment. You need to use your time to make the contribution to this world that you were born to make. That is not to say that social media is a tool that may only be used for distraction. Many people in today's society (including eLIVate) do use social media to spread an important message and to grow their businesses. The idea here is that we want to be in touch with our intention behind using social media. If the intention is to escape from our day-to-day life, we need to ask why we desire that. If the intention is to use it as a tool to maximize our interconnectedness for a higher good, we should continue on our path.

Drugs and Alcohol

Drugs and alcohol are the worst of all distractions. Not only do they take us away from the present moment, they damage us for the future as well. Although we do not engage in any alcohol or drug use, we are not saying you have to take an extreme approach. If you have a glass of wine with dinner and practice moderation, this is not considered a distraction.

You have learned about how to find your true path, how to align yourself with the Light, and how to own the outcomes of your life. This is much more than a new chapter for you – this is a new life. With this new beginning, take a deep breath and enjoy this moment. Allow yourself to align with the Light, and let that feeling come to you and inspire you. Live in alignment. eLIVate your life.

TRUTH

"Truth is by nature self-evident. As soon as you remove the cobwebs of ignorance that surround it, it shines clear."

- Mahatma Gandhi

"I am here for a purpose and that purpose is to grow into a mountain, not to shrink into a grain of sand. Henceforth will I apply all my efforts to become the highest mountain of all and I will train my potential until it cries out for mercy."

– Og Mandino

We believe every person on earth was born knowing that he or she has the intrinsic right, the ability to be happy, and perfectly fulfilled. Many of us have lost this truth through things we have been taught and experiences we have had. When you become re-familiarized with the truth, you are free from suffering, fear and limitation.

We all start from the basics. All human beings are born happy and free. As we have told you before, it has been proven that we are only born with two primal fears—the fear of falling and the fear of loud noises. Logically, it makes sense for us to be born with these fears because in the "wild," we needed them to survive. Even in modern society, these primal fears are still helpful to keep us safe.

After birth, we learn different concepts, values, and ideas from interactions with our family, friends, and teachers. Over time, we assimilate what we are taught into our own belief system. These people are trying to protect us with these teachings. We hear these types of limiting statements all the time, "Don't sit next to an open window, the draft will give you a cold," or, "It is risky to start a business, you should go work for someone else." In these examples, the speaker is coming from a caring place and sharing the only information they know to keep you safe. Since we are connected to those we love, we may not think to question these limiting statements, which lead to our own limiting beliefs. Are there people who sit next to open windows all the time who don't catch a cold? Is going into business for myself really that risky, and if so, risky compared to what?! Instead, we just accept these suggestions and live in accordance with what we are told is "right."

Our teachers have the best of intentions. However, their lessons tend to limit us. The truth is that you have the ability to remain physically healthy in all circumstances, as your mind has a perfect blueprint of your optimal health. You also have the ability to achieve anything you set your mind to and to make those choices based on what is going to make you happy.

The other thing that limits us is the concept of punishment and reward. When we are raised, our parents reward us for our good deeds and punish us when we act out. Over time, we no longer need our parents to reward or punish us. After years of being externally punished and rewarded, we actually assimilate the system of punishment and reward into our own minds, only allowing ourselves joy and reward when we feel we have been good enough and punishing ourselves over and over again when we have made mistakes. The truth of the matter is this—you were born good enough and you do not deserve to be punished.

The most important truth is that we were all born with the same power to direct our outcomes and create our lives. We are all made of the same energy as everything else in the Universe. Since we are connected to this Light energy by our minds, we can tap into and direct this energy based on our thoughts, emotions and actions. Without being aware of their own power, many people walk around today in invisible prisons. They feel trapped in their job, their relationships, or in situations they believe are beyond their control. They do not realize that they have the power to decide what these things mean to them, and change their circumstances. The truth is that you have a choice and you can make that choice right this second.

You are Here for a Purpose

The word purpose is defined as the reason for which something is done or created, or for which something exists. Take a second to think about this. Even if you do not believe in G-d, you must accept that we were created by some kind of force and there must be a reason for having been created. Like your fingerprint, you are unique and have many different facets to your personality. You don't look like, sound like, or act like anyone else on earth. As human beings, our purpose is the reason for which we live exist and this has always been the case.

In the primitive phases of human life, our purpose was to hunt, gather, and survive. We were given instincts to protect us from attack and to help us recognize sources of food. We are also pack animals, meaning we stayed together in a family structure, like we do today. In fact, there is evidence dating back nearly 2 million years, which shows that we lived in familial groups from the very beginning. From this evidence, we can gather the need to be loved developed very early in the stages of human evolution.

We developed a purpose—to survive and to be loved. These basic needs have not left us. Every day, people wake up, get dressed, drive to work, and sit behind a desk for 8 hours to bring food home to the family they love. Although we are no longer hunter-gatherers, the premise is the same. Instead of spending 8 hours hunting for our food in the "wild," we spend 8 hours doing a job for two motivations: survival and love. Even when some people fulfill those basic, primal needs, many of them still feel empty inside. They do not feel fulfilled. They are not excited to spring out of bed in the morning to witness what their day holds. Many of them wake up to an alarm clock and sigh as another long day approaches, just counting the days until Friday when the highly coveted weekend begins. They distract themselves with television, pop culture, alcohol, and other empty activities.

We are sure you have heard stories about or met someone who wakes up, goes to work, comes home, sits down on the couch, cracks open a beer, and watches television. This person may have the same routine for 30-40 working years until they retire. They go through the motions counting down the years, months, and days until their retirement days arrive. They think, "When I retire, then I will be happy." They get to retirement and they are bored and unfulfilled. Why? They are not living a life of purpose and never have.

While we cannot explain why, how, and when humans evolved to want more out of life, we speak from experience when we say humans need more. If you are reading this book, you are certainly seeking something more than you have right now. Even if you are successful by society's standards, you can choose to live a life of significance. We can promise you this, however—distraction does not create a life of significance. When you aren't fulfilled, you may escape into television, pop culture, alcohol, and other vices, which only take you farther and farther away from what you were created to be. In order to tap back into your purpose, these distractions must be eliminated. Only then will your inner voice be heard once again.

This concept can be likened to a GPS or navigation system. When you are about to drive somewhere you have never been, before you can program your GPS/navigation, you have to have an address. If you don't have an exact address, you should at least know a general idea of where you want to go so you can give the GPS some instruction. For example, you may want to type in "gas station" or "hotel." You are programming your GPS with purpose. Once you have programmed the GPS and you set out on the road, if you miss a turn or a highway exit, the GPS will recalculate your route. It will do this as many times as is necessary to ensure that you reach your desired destination.

Life is just like this. The Light is like the Universe's GPS, guiding us and showing us the path to our dreams. However, if we do not have a purpose, we cannot take the first step. We cannot program our minds and create the maps to where we want to go. Without direction, it is easy to get lost and even drive around in circles.

This is why purpose is the most important concept taught in this book. Every other technique, exercise, and theory will only be effective if utilized with your purpose in mind. Without it you can have all of the tools, strategies, and techniques in the world and never make a change in the right direction.

The exercises below will help you identify your purpose, which will be the "North" on your compass. Your North will always be the place where you are inspired and filled with love. It will never be a place of fear or apprehension. Eventually, you will develop an instinct that tells you whether your compass is pointed in the right direction. If it isn't, you will find your "North" and re-think your route. You can simply ask, "Is what I am doing right now getting me closer to, or farther away from my chosen destiny?"

For some people, their purpose calls out so loudly they feel as though they have absolutely no choice but to listen. These are the people who may have a natural talent or inclination and start on their journey early in life. These are the people some watch from a distance and say they are lucky, or they got dealt a "good hand." Those who find their purpose early are fortunate, but they are fundamentally no different from you.

You are meant to have a purpose, too, you are simply still searching, and that is perfectly fine. In the end, the search is part of the journey. When you have found your purpose and are on course, you will look back and realize all of the pieces of your past have come together to make you exactly who you are today—the person with all of the skills that make you capable of pursuing your true path. The person who is ready to make it happen always will.

Some of the people who contribute to our world most are not the people who were given the most resources. They are not usually the people who have been given the best education, or showered with love. The people who contribute the most are those who have had to experience adversity, challenges, and a great deal of pain to become who they are. The pain they experienced has given them a deep desire to make a change. It has also changed their outlook on life to make them more compassionate, open, and loving.

Think about all the people we have shared with you in this book. You already know how much they have been through to become the people they are today. These stories only scratch the surface. There are far more people and too many stories to share. Every triumph and every success has come through learning who they were by moving through challenges, and rising to meet those challenges over and over again.

What Adversity Can Mean to You

There are many stories of people who have moved through adversity and come out on the other side with a life of purpose. For example, the woman who was raped and later becomes an attorney who prosecutes rapists. The man whose father dies of medical complications becomes a lifesaving surgeon working in the emergency room. The entrepreneur who grew up with poor parents, who were unable to provide for him and his siblings, now runs a multi-million dollar company.

Nona's purpose was uncovered just like this. As a young child, she lost her younger brother to medical complications. As a little girl, she wasn't even able to comprehend the idea of death. She kept asking her parents why her brother went away and didn't come back. She became a silent observer during this time. As a child not able to understand death and grief, Nona watched her parents mourn the loss of their child. She watched endless tears, self-blame, and sadness overtake her family. She found herself wanting to fix the situation. She wanted to reach into her parents' hearts and heal them. This is how she began to evolve into the healer she is today.

The other lesson from this experience was even more powerful. As a little girl, she came to the realization we are given one life on this earth and that we are not guaranteed a single moment. To Nona, this meant that you must maximize each and every moment. You must drain every drop of purpose from your life that you can. Through this, Nona developed the drive to heal others and help them experience a shift in perspective. She wanted to live in a way that would inspire others to recognize the gift of life and how to be grateful for it each step of the way.

Stories like these are endless because the adversity these people experienced forced them to go inward to the core of who they were, and find a reason to live. Many times this is how people find out their reason for being is to help others. Giving and receiving are part of life's cycle.

There is a very relevant quote that speaks about how adversity can help you find your purpose that says, "Once the storm is over, you won't remember how you made it through, how you managed to survive. You won't even be sure, whether the storm is really over. One thing is certain. When you come out of the storm, you won't be the same person who walked in. That's what this storm's all about." The point is adversity teaches us about ourselves. It forces us into a position where we must be more resourceful than we have ever been emotionally, financially, and otherwise. Adversity teaches us what we are made of and who we are. Many people who are inspired to change this world do so because of a personal experience of their own. These experiences give people a deep desire for change that cannot be artificially created. The desire is backed by the strongest forms of human emotion, and nothing is more powerful.

You must remember you always have a choice. Even when the choices presented to you seem difficult, they are still yours. When faced with adversity, there are two options. One option is to grow and allow the experience to mold you into a stronger person who finds passion because of your journey. The other is to become a victim of the experience. The two are mutually exclusive. Always choose passion. Choose to take back the driver's seat in your life.

You Make Your Own Luck

There are other types of people who make huge impacts on society, and their paths have unfolded in a way that makes others view them as lucky. We believe that luck is created in the mind; thus, we will use an example of how people looking in may see luck, while those on the inside are creating opportunities. In the book Outliers, Malcolm Gladwell writes about the Beatles and how they got the chance to acquire the 10,000 hours necessary for mastery of their art. They were working in a cafe and were asked to come back and perform every day. As a result of their daily performances, they were able to accumulate the 10,000 hours of practice that many say is required to become a master. People looking from the outside may say, "The Beatles got lucky when they landed that gig." Those who have come across opportunities know they make their own luck.

Before The Beatles got the opportunity to play their music nightly, they had already been focused on music and the success of their band. They had already trained their brains, though inadvertently, to recognize opportunities that would get them closer to their goals. They had also put that energy into the Universe that delivered by bringing the opportunity forth. The Beatles lived a life of purpose and by the time that opportunity came to pass, they were already moving forward on their path. They were already focused. Opportunities do not drop into the laps of those who have not pointed their thoughts in that direction. They come to those who have focused their thoughts and aligned their intentions with their higher purpose.

Creating Your Path to Purpose

You may be asking yourself, if I wasn't born certain of my purpose, and I haven't been exposed to an earth-shattering amount of adversity, then how to I find my purpose? The answer is within you, but if you are not used to listening to your inner voice then it will be difficult to hear.

Before you start this exercise, make a commitment to yourself right here, right now.

"I ____________, promise to openly accept the challenge of finding my purpose. I am willing to do the soul searching it will take to find out why I was created. I will journal, meditate, and seek support if necessary. I will never, never give up."

Signature: ______________________________

Date: ______________________________

Now that you have made this commitment to yourself you can start to uncover your calling. It is there, we promise.

1. Think back to a time (even if this was early childhood), where you felt happy. What were you doing? This could be drawing, writing, climbing trees, etc.
2. List the roles you currently hold in your own life and next to the role you list, write the significance of that role.
   Role:
   Ex: Mother
   Significance:
   Love and care for others
3. List 10 things you feel that you are good at. These can be anything. Don't judge yourself—just write. Every talent counts no matter how silly you think you are when you do practice or perform them.
4. In what causes do you believe?

5. If you had one week to live, what are twenty things you would need to accomplish before you die?
6. If you could wake up and do anything tomorrow, what would it be?

Now that you have begun uncovering your purpose you can use the following principals and concepts to help you set goals that allow you to live your purpose and harness the powers within you.

Steps to Finding Purpose

1. Think back to childhood. What did you want to be back then? This is often very telling because even if the image of the exact profession has changed since then, the intention may not have. For example, someone who wanted to be a nurse or a doctor may have wanted this due to a deep desire to care for others. This can take the shape of many different paths in that person's life.
2. Ask yourself what you would do today if you could do anything. Be honest, even though we appreciate that this can be a difficult question. You will be surprised what answers you get when you listen.

Once you have an idea of your purpose, begin to form a vision of your purpose. Focus in on it. Once you change your focus, you are more likely to become inspired by your own thoughts or the world around you. Keep in mind that you must remain open to receiving inspiration. It can come in many forms. It can be in art, music, or meeting another person whose story inspires you. Choose to be open and allow yourself to follow the path that begins to unfold from this moment on.

Your Nature is That of a Creative Being

Despite our individual unique qualities, we do share some similarities. We all need oxygen, food, water, and sleep to survive. We all seek happiness in our own way. Most of us like to have some kind of desire to live a life of purpose. Just like our needs as human beings are very similar, our abilities are very similar.

Take a moment to reflect on our similarities. Now, imagine an ocean. When you think of the ocean as a whole, you know that it is vast and powerful. Each drop of water, however, is made up of the same components as the whole. The Universe is a creative and powerful force of which we are all a part, just like the drop of water in the ocean. Therefore, it follows that as a part of this greater whole (the Universe), we are both creative and powerful.

You see, the Universe is an ecosystem. Every process, every system, and every animal is connected to the whole and each exists for a specific reason. Evolution teaches us that humans and other animals have adapted to become fit for survival. None of the species had to consciously think "Hmmm, I don't need to have that extra toe anymore ... why don't I get rid of it." Instead, the intelligence of the Universe causes the animal to change over time for the purpose of better suiting it for its environment. There is intelligence like this all around us. Every day there are birds flying in formation, bees pollinating flowers, baby animals feeding from their mother's breast, and packs of hunting animals identifying their prey by spotting their weaknesses. These qualities were not taught. They are innate. We are part of an intelligent, magnificent and creative Universe.

Like the water drop is connected to the ocean through its elements, we, as humans are connected to the Universe. Humans, however, have been given a unique gift—thought. It is our mind that connects us to the Universe and allows us to be creative. To understand how this power works, we must first understand the component parts of our mind and the significance each part has in our lives.

Consciousness, Generally

Many people think that consciousness is all we are; it stops or shuts off when we sleep. This is not the case. Now, we are sure that you have had the experience of being woken up by someone calling your name. You could be in the soundest sleep, but as soon as your name is called you mysteriously wake up. This is because you are conscious when you are asleep, even if that consciousness takes place at varying levels.

The "Conscious Mind"

The conscious mind is the part of your mind that you are familiar with. This is the part of your mind that engages you with thoughts, feelings, and emotions. You may catch yourself thinking, "It is warm outside." This is a conscious observation. As the rational part of your mind, the conscious mind is responsible for logical thinking, and for providing the subconscious mind with directions. Therefore, it is very important to monitor and control your thoughts because your conscious thoughts end up as the instructions that your subconscious mind will follow.

The "Subconscious Mind"

Unlike the conscious mind, your subconscious mind is not rational. It has no ability to discern between good and bad, right and wrong, lack and abundance, etc. The primary function of the subconscious mind is to carry out the orders given by your conscious mind. It is also responsible for maintaining your physical health. Your subconscious mind is the force responsible for operating all of your vital organs. This is why you do not have to make your heart beat and the reason why your body continues to function perfectly—even while asleep.

A good way to draw the distinction between the two minds is to imagine a ship captain. The captain gives directions to the crew members and they obey without question. If the captain's directions are incorrect, the ship may crash, as the crew members merely carry out the orders they receive. They do not question. Just like this, your subconscious mind will go to work immediately upon receiving direction from your conscious mind, no questions asked.

How to Get the Conscious and Subconscious to Work in Unison

Again, the formula for effective thinking is **desire + emotion + thought = outcome**. This means that when you desire something, if you back that desire with emotion, and think about that thing, you can create it. It is important to be careful here. Both desire and emotion can be good or bad. Remember, your mind does not process the words "do not" or "cannot." Therefore, you may have a strong desire not to have a certain outcome or circumstance, and manifest it by accident. For example, if you say, "I don't want to end up poor," your mind hears "end up poor." This desire is coupled with a strong emotion—fear. You end up manifesting the exact opposite of what you want! Therefore, the first point to take away is that you must tell your mind what you want specifically and clearly. Your new profanity words are don't, can't, and impossible. Stop using those words!

Next, timing is important. Your subconscious mind is most receptive to messaging and imagery when your brain is in alpha or theta state. Generally, your subconscious mind is more open to direction when you are relaxed. Research indicates that this time is first thing in the morning when you wake up, and right before you go to bed at night. Therefore, use this time to say your affirmations, read over your goals, and think about your desired outcomes.

Third, create a vision board. Imagery greatly helps the subconscious grasp what you want. Images are specific and easy to absorb. You can create your vision board any way you like. You can make a traditional vision board on poster board using magazine cut outs, or you can create a virtual vision board. The important part of this exercise is to end up with a visual representation of things that make you happy; the things you want out of life.

Fourth, visualize. Think about achieving your goals and visualize them in your mind. Lie down and get into a relaxed state. Visualize yourself in the job you desire. Imagine every component of your work day: driving to the office, walking in to greet your co-workers, catching up with your colleagues at the coffee machine, sitting at your desk. Research conducted on athletes reveals the same part of the brain that is activated during visualization (dorsolateral prefrontal cortex) is also activated during the same activity in real life. For example, a basketball player imagining shooting a basketball is using the same part of the brain he uses when he is actually shooting the ball. This means that your brain cannot tell the difference. In other words, your brain does not know whether you are imagining something is happening or whether it is actually happening. This allows you to program your brain with the reality you want. Visualization is a powerful tool. Visualize what you want until you have it.

Finally, remember to start and end each day with gratitude. The more you feel something, the more you will attract of that same thing. Take the time to count your blessings. You can write them down on a piece of paper, or use a gratitude rock. No matter what method you choose to accomplish this, make sure that you actually feel grateful when you count your blessings. This is not an exercise you do to "go through the motions." The more you are grateful, the more you will have to be grateful for.

Remember, these are the first steps to getting your conscious mind and subconscious mind in alignment with where you want to be. For these to work, you must have your purpose in mind and you must be consistent. If you have a lot of negative beliefs in place, you will also have to do some work to get to the root of those beliefs and re-shape how you view the world. Your beliefs are like a map and they may be misguiding you.

When you study the concept of the mind as a creative force, there are a few important points to understand. First, your mind connects you to the creative force in the Universe. It allows you to be one with the whole. Second, your mind, although one mind, it has two interconnected parts—your conscious mind and your subconscious mind. Your conscious mind gives directions. Your subconscious mind carries out any and all directions given, whether those directions are positive or negative. You must understand that monitoring your thoughts allows you to monitor the creative process and therefore control your results.

Now that you understand our human relationship to the Universe, and the way to harness thought, take a moment to complete a brief exercise:

1. What is one specific outcome you desire in life? This can be anything (job, car, spouse, etc.), but you must be very specific when you list it. When you write this down, be descriptive. Fully write out each quality that you want the thing or person to have.
2. What do you believe about your relationship to this outcome now? Do you believe it is possible? Is it in your reach?

3. If you answered "no," list what you will have to believe in order to achieve that outcome.
4. Make a list of action steps. This is an action map that will take you, in steps, from where you are right now to where you want to be. Since the Universe will provide you with many of these steps, you do not have to be extremely specific here. Just write down the basic steps. For example, if you desire a job, you may have to complete your resume and do some research, etc. Whatever those are, write them down.

You have found ways to discover your inner purpose and find the truth you have been carrying around with you from the moment you were born. The Universe, us, and the Light don't care if you are 8 or 80 when you find this truth. We just want you to find it. We want you to not just live, but to thrive in the life that was given to you no matter what your obstacles are. Remember, everyone is given things that will stand in their way and no one ever has an easy road. Do not spend your time wishing to be someone else. You were given a gift so rare and precious that if you follow the inner Light we have been teaching you to use as your compass, you'll find the passion that has been begging you find it since your first day on earth. Live your Truth, eLIVate your life.

EMPOWERMENT

> *"We delight in the beauty of the butterfly, but rarely admit the changes it has gone through to achieve that beauty."*
>
> — *Maya Angelou*

Empowerment comes from inner transformation. To be empowered, you must understand the relationship between your thoughts and the circumstances in your life. You must align your thoughts with your dreams, hopes, and desires.

Once you have read this, you will have learned the relationship between energy, love, inspiration, vision, alignment, and truth. No matter who you are or where you come from, you have the right to be free and control your outcomes. When you understand this, you will walk around with a lot more personal power than you would if you felt like things just happened to you. The key is, you must use the tools in this book and you must constantly strive to continue to master them. The journey is wonderful and the world is full of opportunities to learn and grow. If you don't seize the opportunities, you will be trapped on the treadmill running full speed to nowhere until you are exhausted and have nothing to show for it.

You have the choice to become empowered. Inside you is a person who is strong, who can fight for your dreams, and who was put here for a very specific purpose. It is time to own that. Once you do, you will start to feel that things are falling into place. It's not magic. It is what you have carefully directed your energy toward.

Here is an Exercise to Help You on Your Journey to Empowerment

Think back to a time in your life when you felt in control of an outcome. This can be any event or circumstance and it can have happened at any point in your life. Maybe you wanted to earn an A on a test and you studied very hard and achieved that goal. Maybe you were a high school or college athlete who prepared for a big game and won. These were times you were empowered. You had an end goal in mind, and you focused on it. You held that vision in your mind and heart, you took the action necessary, and you achieved your goal. Now, write that instance down on a sheet of paper. Describe it in detail and try to remember all the details of what you saw, heard, and felt during that time.

Recognize you can bring that feeling back in any area of your life. You can feel that deep sense of pride and accomplishment every day. You can feel that feeling in your relationship, at work, or in any circumstance you direct your attention on. You must only choose to feel that.

Next, take the time to write down a situation where you would like to feel empowered right now. This can be a baby step. It can be a small goal you have been trying to achieve lately, or it can be more expansive and long-term. This is your journey and it is up to you. Write that goal down and make it specific. Remember, specific goals are easier for your mind to execute upon. Finally, create a vision around that goal and feeling of empowerment.

Once you have taken these steps you will be amazed at what you accomplish. The path to achieving your goals will unfold, and you will be on your way to an empowering life. There is a reason that we chose to make empowered action the last step in our system. You can understand everything else, but if you fail to *act* you may not receive the end results you want. This is where the rubber meets the road. How do you begin to take empowered action?

GOALS AND AFFIRMATIONS

Goals

We were once taught the difference between a dream and a goal—you dream a dream and you write down the goal. That's all there is to it. The caveat is you must write the goal correctly. Writing a goal is part intuition, part art, and part science. Before we teach you how to write an effective goal, let's define this term first. A goal is defined as "an end toward which effort is directed." This definition is important, because as we discussed earlier, your internal navigation system cannot guide you without specific direction. What is an effective goal made of?

First, you must start with your why. Your, "why" is the reason you seek to create something. According to our alignment pyramid, your why originates at the spiritual level. You become inspired to achieve something and you start to feel passionate about it. Remember, goals come in all shapes and sizes. Even small goals have come to us for a specific reason—to help us evolve. Therefore, each goal must be honored and treated as though it is just as important as our larger goals. There are no small miracles.

Ask yourself the following: "Why am I trying to achieve this goal?" When you know the reason behind your inspired action, the motivation to accomplish the goal is much stronger. Here is an example of a goal without a why: I want to lose 20 pounds. Here is the same goal, but with the underlying motivation added: I want to lose 20 pounds to become more healthy, to stabilize my blood sugar, to lower my blood pressure, and to stay alive for my family for many years to come. When you want to lose 20 pounds to increase your overall health and therefore your lifespan to spend more time with the people you love, you are a lot more compelled to achieve that weight loss. Therefore, goal writing tip #1 is write your "why" directly into your goal.

Second, think about present tense vs. pushing your goal out into the future. Many people write goals as though they are yet to occur. The future tense wording of the goal signals it has not occurred. In the eyes of your subconscious mind, this means that the goal is out in the future. Your subconscious mind has no concept of time. It is merely a servant that will carry out the orders from your conscious mind. Therefore, for optimal effectiveness, your goals must be written in present tense. Here is an example of a future tense goal: I plan to lose 20 pounds over the course of four months. Here is the same goal, but in the present tense: It is now July 4, 2015 and I weigh 125 pounds (goal weight). You see, if you continue to say, "I will start tomorrow" or push your goals out into the future, your subconscious will continue pushing your goals out further and further into the future. You must convey that the goal "already is." If you believe that you can achieve it, it is already so. Write it that way!

Third, think about your goal in relationship to the big picture. When we write our goals, we have some that are more immediate, and some that are part of the grand vision for our lives. You should have some larger theme type goals as well as some stepping-stones.

Affirmations

Many self-help books talk about affirmations and how they are the "be all, end all." This can be true in some cases, but only if the person is in full alignment to begin with. You see, you can't just cover up deep-rooted fears, insecurities, and limiting beliefs by attempting to drown them in endless hours of affirmations. This can only result in more internal conflict. The key to having affirmations work for you is to ensure you are living from a place of faith and not fear to begin with. At that point, affirmations become reinforcement to your already established connection with your highest self.

We have already addressed fear in depth. We have taught you why fear arises and how to tackle it on your own. The last thing that is worth mentioning is that you have full control over your fears because they begin with thoughts. Before you can choose to be afraid of something (assuming it is not flight or fight and that you have time to react), you first have to decide what it means to you. For example, if you are about to give a big presentation, you can choose that it will be a terrifying experience or an effortless, smooth experience. This is an agreement that you make with yourself ahead of time. The reaction that you have during the presentation itself is a manifestation of the agreement you made with yourself far before the presentation actually occurred. To live from a place of faith, not fear is a choice. You must choose to make a new agreement with yourself. Be calm, not afraid.

If you have followed the other steps outlined in this book, you will already understand your relationship to the outcomes in your life, and you will be well on your way to living in full alignment. Once you feel you are living these principles, it is time to write your affirmations. Here is how you start:

1. Go back through the life purpose exercise. Make sure you are really clear on what you are trying to accomplish. More importantly, be extremely clear on why you are trying to achieve it.
2. Go back through the vision exercise. You will want to have your vision at the top of your mind prior to writing your affirmation.
3. Start with the words "I am." These words are proven to be the most powerful affirming words there are. Sometimes, we need to escape from the world of over thinking and just "be." This means we must consciously act to remove the resistance from our thoughts and allow our highest self to come through us like a channel of energy. Stating the words "I am" first instructs your subconscious mind that

the condition you are affirming is in the present moment, and second, sends a strong message to the Universe that this must happen quickly.

4. Now craft your affirmation. Like writing a goal, this process is part art, part science. Here is an example: "I am a living example of the abundance in the Universe."

If you write your affirmation down and feel a sense of incongruence, you need to back track through the previous steps. You can also take yourself down a slower path with your affirmations. If you write yours down and hear a voice saying "I don't believe that about myself", then try re-wording your affirmation as follows: "I am in the process of attracting the perfect job." Your mind can't dispute that you are in the process of achieving something. This may make the message more acceptable to your conscious mind. The acceptance will then translate into your subconscious and start getting you results.

Successful people have been using what you have been reading in this book for ages. They have found ways to follow their inner compass and were led by the same Light that is inside each and every one of us. They know how to take action and follow their dreams by creating goals that focus on the present. Other than their ability to channel their energy, however, these people are just like you.

Think of star athletes like LeBron James. If you have ever watched him play you'll hear his team mates refer to a thing they call "beast mode." James uses empowered action to focus on his goal—getting the ball into the basket every time he touches it. He makes it his job to get that ball either for himself or his teammates at all costs. This is what we mean by empowered action. Follow your goal until it's the only thing you see. The moment you look away and see all the obstacles in your way is the moment you'll lose focus on your desired outcome. To succeed at something, you must focus only on your North.

If you want a career, take action. If you want to be a world-renowned speaker like Tony Robbins, practice speaking in front of crowds. Even if only 4 people show up, speak to them like they are a group of 400. If you want to write a book, get a blank book and cut and paste what you'll want your cover to be like and put it together. Put it on your desk and look at it while you write your book as a reminder of your goal. Create a physical compass for what you want to attain and you'll create your very own beast mode. Empower yourself now, eLIVate your life.

Conclusion

Our hope is that, through the words of this book, you have been transformed. Life is always a journey. There is a saying that no man ever steps into the same river twice. This is because the man has changed and the river has changed. When you pick this book up again, you will be different than you were the first time you read it. You may be at a completely different place in your life, allowing you to assign a totally new meaning to its words and exercises. Sometimes, you may want to pick it up at random and see what page opens up to you. This is an exercise we use with our favorite books when we need guidance or direction. We open the book and trust that the Light has guided us to the message we need, when we need it. This is another way of communicating to our source.

Each and every word in this book was written with pure love. Prior to placing these words on the page, we set the intention that this book would be used to change the world for the better. As each reader has a unique purpose for their life, we hope that this book will allow that to blossom. Through this, the world is changed through one thought, one person, and one empowered action at a time. We will leave you with this guided meditation. You can read this aloud or to yourself. If you are having trouble embracing any of the chapters feel free to write the parts of the mediation below to be constant reminders for you or to use as your own affirmations

Energy

I recognize that, like all of my brothers and sisters, I am made of Light. I was born with the ability to use the Light in a loving way by channeling my thoughts and my actions toward my highest purpose. At all times, I choose to emanate peace, love, and Light in my vibrational bubble.

Love

I choose now to forgive myself and others for past mistakes. I, in this very moment, start over with a clean slate. I allow love and Light into my heart, and have full faith that as I love myself, I draw more love into my experience. I trust that any and all healing that I need, will begin with the love I choose to accept into my experience now.

Inspiration

As a unique and creative being, I open myself to the messages from the Light. I allow the Light to communicate with me, so I may share my special gifts with the world. I commit to allowing this inspiration's voice to be heard, through whatever medium necessary for me to receive that message. I commit to removing energetic blocks that may stop my inspiration from fully expressing in my experience.

I promise to use my inspiration to make my own personal dent in the Universe.

Vision

I accept that the vision I choose to hold in my mind will begin to manifest in my experience. I choose to focus my vision on my desired outcome, rather than the potential obstacles that may arise. I promise to honor my vision and hold it close to my heart, as I know that this vision was given so I may impact this world for good.

Alignment

I set my intention on full alignment. When I become inspired from my higher self, I vow to honor that inspiration through my thoughts, feelings and actions. I understand that my relationship to my physical outcomes depends on the thoughts and feelings I allow into my daily experience hour-by-hour and day-by-day. I understand that I have the power to choose to revoke negative thoughts and emotions at any moment. I choose to only embrace thoughts and emotions that align with my highest purpose for my life on earth. I promise to live my values, such that I can set a loving example for those around me to live within their purpose. I will act according to my beliefs, spreading love and kindness wherever I go and always where it is needed by my brothers and sisters.

Truth

I know that I am here for a purpose. My purpose is to grow to be the person that is ready and able to fully express my genuine and unique talents and gifts. I will be grateful for and honor my uniqueness, as I know that there is no one else on earth that is just like me. I will walk in my truth each day, ensuring that each step forward will get me closer to my vision and my chosen path. I will allow only the beliefs that align with my highest self. I will observe my thoughts and beliefs such that I choose to accept the loving thoughts and beliefs about myself. I will leave all other thoughts and beliefs outside of my experience, letting them go without judgment.

Empowerment

I understand that I am made of energy. I have been given a unique gift that allows me to choose my thoughts and therefore my experience. I know that I can direct my energy through my thoughts, desire, and emotions. I will love all people and all things with all of my heart. Therefore, I will express gratitude each day. I will listen for inspiration from the Light, which I know will always send me on my highest path. I will align myself with my highest purpose with my thoughts and emotions. I will always remember my truth, holding it close to my heart and protecting it despite outside conditions and circumstances. When I do this, I am empowered. I will walk with certainty knowing I am living from a place of purpose and contribution to this world. I am able to do anything and everything through love, faith, and courage. I am empowered.

Remember, you are different than anyone else on earth. You are here to fulfill a specific purpose that no one else can perform. You are the only one able to hear the messages from the Light about what that purpose is and how it will take form in your experience. If each person lived out their true purpose and chose love in every interaction with others, our world would be totally transformed. Mankind would regain their freedom from lack, restraint, limitations, and from the ideals that have been set for us by society. Let your Light by your compass. eLIVate your Life!

About The Authors

Lani Baron, Esq. and Nona Djavid, D.C., are the founders of eLIVate Institute.

Lani was led to the Light after a long personal journey initiated by her parents' high conflict divorce, her mother's struggle with addiction, and her sister's death. These experiences left Lani feeling alone in the world without a sense of belonging. This inspired Lani to seek the truth, and when she found it the direction of her entire life changed. Nona's fascination with the Light began at the age of 15, when she stumbled upon a handful of books about spirituality, personal growth, and creative visualization. From that point forward, Nona started paving her own destiny full of abundance and success utilizing years of study and techniques she learned growing up.

Lani, an attorney, founded Alternative Divorce Solutions, which is a divorce mediation practice with locations in Newport Beach, Long Beach, and Los Angeles. Nona, a chiropractor, has established four successful businesses before the age of 30. Both women chose their first careers with the desire to help others.

After accomplishing these goals, the authors realized that their vision expanded much further than their current professions could reach. They wanted to change the world by changing the consciousness of the masses. Both women recognized that our consciousness shapes both our personal experiences and our collective experiences, as we are all one in the Universe. They wanted to raise this awareness in others to make a positive impact in the world. This is how eLIVate was born. eLIVate is a collection of the threads of wisdom the authors have collected through their personal experiences and individual connections to the Light. It is the authors' hope that the words in this book will reach into your heart and light your way.

Printed in the United States
By Bookmasters